LEAD *like* CHRIST

Books by A.W. Tozer

COMPILED AND EDITED BY JAMES L. SNYDER

Alive in the Spirit

And He Dwelt Among Us

A Cloud by Day, a Fire by Night

The Crucified Life

The Dangers of a Shallow Faith

Delighting in God

A Disruptive Faith

The Essential Tozer Collection 3-in-1

Experiencing the Presence of God

The Fire of God's Presence

God's Power for Your Life

Lead like Christ

Living as a Christian

My Daily Pursuit

No Greater Love

Preparing for Jesus' Return

The Purpose of Man

The Pursuit of God

The Quotable Tozer

Reclaiming Christianity

Voice of a Prophet

The Wisdom of God

BOOKS BY JAMES L. SNYDER

The Life of A.W. Tozer: In Pursuit of God—The Authorized Biography

LEAD *like* CHRIST

REFLECTING THE QUALITIES AND CHARACTER OF CHRIST IN YOUR MINISTRY

A.W. TOZER

COMPILED AND EDITED BY JAMES L. SNYDER

Published by Bethany House Publishers
11400 Hampshire Avenue South
Minneapolis, Minnesota 55438
www.bethanyhouse.com

Bethany House Publishers is a division of
Baker Publishing Group, Grand Rapids, Michigan

Printed in the United States of America

Library of Congress Cataloging-in-Publication Data

Names: Tozer, A. W. (Aiden Wilson), 1897-1963, author. | Snyder, James L., editor. | Tozer, A. W. (Aiden Wilson), 1897-1963. Sermons. Selections.

Title: Lead like Christ : reflecting the qualities and character of Christ in your ministry / A.W. Tozer, James L. Snyder.

Description: Minneapolis, Minnesota : Bethany House, a division of Baker Publishing Group, [2021] | "Based upon a series of sermons on the book of Titus"—Introduction.

Identifiers: LCCN 2020058110 | ISBN 9780764239106 (casebound) | ISBN 9780764234033 (trade paperback) | ISBN 9781493431687 (ebook)

Subjects: LCSH: Jesus Christ—Leadership. | Bible. Titus—Criticism, interpretation, etc. | Christian leadership. | Pastoral theology.

Classification: LCC BV652.1 .T685 2021 | DDC 253—dc23

LC record available at https://lccn.loc.gov/2020058110

Cover design by Rob Williams, InsideOut Creative Arts, Inc.

James L. Snyder is represented by The Steve Laube Agency.

Baker Publishing Group publications use paper produced from sustainable forestry practices and post-consumer waste whenever possible.

24 25 26 27 8 7 6 5 4

CONTENTS

Introduction 7

1. Lead like Christ: The Foundation 9
2. Lead like Christ: The Model 17
3. Lead like Christ: A Demonstration 27
4. Lead like Christ: Motivated by the Complete Truth 35
5. Lead like Christ: The Framework of God's Promises 47
6. Lead like Christ: Manifested through Preaching 55
7. Lead like Christ: Understanding Biblical Order 63
8. Lead like Christ: The Obvious Fruit 71
9. Lead like Christ: Attributes of a Spiritual Leader 81
10. Lead like Christ: Understanding the Threefold Qualification 89
11. Lead like Christ: Maintaining a Tight Grip on the Word 97

12. Lead like Christ: A Commitment to Sound Doctrine 107
13. Lead like Christ: Teaching the Attributes of God's Grace 115
14. Lead like Christ: Our True Value to Christ 125
15. Lead like Christ: The Fullness of Christian Leadership 135
16. Lead like Christ: How God Sees Us 143
17. Lead like Christ: The Christ-Centered Servant 153
18. Lead like Christ: Our Motives Reveal Christ's Character in Us 163
19. Lead like Christ: Facing Spiritual Warfare 171

Conclusion 181

INTRODUCTION

Reading a Tozer book can be quite a challenge. Throughout his ministry, he never focused on weak Christians who were only after the pleasures of life.

The audience Tozer focused on were those with an incurable hunger and thirst for the deep things of God. In chapter 15, for example, he essentially says only Christians with backbone will ever get into heaven. Of course, what he meant was that our Christianity has to be such that we stand against everything contrary to the nature of Jesus Christ.

If we are going to be servants of Christ, we need to be Christlike in every regard.

One quote I like from Tozer is "God does not call the equipped. Rather, in His wisdom, God equips the called." That seems to be the underlying message in this book.

Throughout his ministry, Tozer was never hesitant about offending people. He did not do it unnecessarily or because he had a mean spirit. Quite the opposite. He knew that some of the things he was teaching and writing about would not be acceptable to immature and carnal Christians. And sure enough, his teaching did offend them because it did not fit into their spiritual agenda.

This book is based on a series of sermons on the book of Titus. In this series, Tozer used Paul's advice to Titus to guide those of us today who want to serve Christ acceptably.

This is not an inspirational book to help spiritual leaders feel good about themselves. Consider it a workbook to empower men and women to be the kinds of leaders needed by the church today. To drive them to their knees in absolute surrender.

Sound doctrine is so essential that Tozer does not write to CEOs but rather to people akin to CTOs (chief theological officers). That is why he spends time dealing with theological issues that Paul established for Titus. One concern Tozer had was that many spiritual leaders are doctrinally challenged.

Tozer's emphasis is that we are to lead like Christ, which requires a thorough understanding of biblical doctrine. Too often people focus on certain issues and divide the church into little doctrinal clubs.

The challenge Tozer gives is to follow the real Jesus—the Jesus of the New Testament—and be prepared to be treated like Christ was treated in His day.

Like with other Tozer books, you will not be able to read this in one sitting. It will take time to process the truth he shares in these pages. Yet I believe, and it happened to me, that this book will give you a new perspective on what it means to be a spiritual leader.

Dr. James L. Snyder

1

Lead like Christ
THE FOUNDATION

That I may know Him and the power of His resurrection, and the fellowship of His sufferings, being conformed to His death, if, by any means, I may attain to the resurrection from the dead.

Philippians 3:10–11

Many are interested in what we call ministry. Yet, my heart saddens to realize that many do not understand what spiritual ministry is all about from the biblical point of view. For some reason, we have brought into the church the world's business methods to fulfill Christ's call.

A journey through the Gospels will show the passion Christ had when it came to ministry. He completely rejected the world and even religion to minister to the people around Him.

I am not against education. But I do feel many people are too educated, and by that I mean they are educated beyond their ability to function in the spiritual world. They are trapped in techniques and methods.

If secular education were absolutely necessary for ministry, that would rule me out. After my first day of eighth grade, I came home from school and told my mother that I could do a better job than my teacher. I never returned to school, and instead spent most of my time in the library reading books. It was perhaps a little arrogant of me, but I eventually got over it.

Education is important; but where it's coming from and how we handle it matters.

A friend of mine used to say, "Get as much education as you can and earn as many degrees as possible, and then when you're all finished, lay it on the altar and give it over to God. If God uses it, great. If God does not use that education, that is His choice."

Christ, the Key to Ministry

This book is not a book of techniques and methods—a book that could be titled something like *10 Keys to a Successful Ministry*. That would be how a worldly minded person would approach it. There is only one key to ministry: Christ.

When Abraham laid Isaac on the altar, it must have seemed like the most horrendous thing he had ever done in his relationship with God. Isaac represented everything Abraham had worked for, and now God wanted him to lay his son on the altar. Yet when Abraham did it without reservation, God gave Isaac back in a way that Abraham never could have imagined.

> *It is the Holy Spirit, and nothing else, who energizes our spiritual leadership.*

When we lay our education, experience, and expectations on the altar and give our ministry over to God without reservation, and are even willing to walk away from it, then God in His power can give what He wants us to have.

God does not call the equipped. Rather, in His wisdom, God equips the called. And that's where the power and authority of God flow in the life of the servant. The equipping of God's servant is a wonder that flows from heaven, and nothing on earth can hinder it.

In no way is biblical ministry associated with business. Business techniques of the world cannot accomplish the goals of spiritual leadership. When we use the world's methods, we push aside the work of the Holy Spirit. It is the Holy Spirit, and nothing else, who runs and energizes our spiritual leadership. To grieve the Holy Spirit is to jeopardize the true ministry of Christ.

Whenever God moves, He pushes aside the world, and the focus is on Christ. The world cannot honor Christ—only the true church can.

I'm not sure a church's size has anything to do with this, but I've noticed that the bigger the church, the more it relies on worldly and business methods.

If we are going to lead like Christ, we need to model our leadership after His and observe how He dealt with the issues of His day. At the time, His main opposition was religion. The religious people and leaders did not want anything to do with Jesus. They considered Him a danger to their religiosity and lifestyle.

The government also opposed Jesus, and when the Pharisees tried to get Jesus to choose sides between religion and Rome, He responded, "'Render to Caesar the things that are Caesar's, and to God the things that are God's.' And they marveled at Him" (Mark 12:17).

When Jesus walked on water, it was a great illustration that He never allowed worldly circumstances to determine what He was going to do or not do. (Remember what happened to Peter when he tried to walk on water? He became obsessed with the circumstances and fell in.)

In this book, my purpose is to focus on how you and I, as servants of Christ, can lead like Christ in the circumstances we are in today. My focus will be on the book of Titus, which records how Paul mentored Titus to be a model servant and lead like Christ.

The Foundation of Spiritual Leadership

But before we go further, what is the foundation for all of this? On what do we build our spiritual leadership?

Again, is it education? Is it experience? Is it adopting the world's methods?

No, it is none of that. Thus, we need to clearly understand what we build our ministry upon. I want to say right here that every born-again Christian is involved in ministry. We are not called to do the same kind of ministry as our brother or sister. But all of us, together, are engaged in the ministry of Jesus Christ.

Every born-again Christian is involved in ministry.

To lead like Christ, the first thing we need to do is to *know Christ*. This is a crucial element of spiritual leadership.

Now, if I were to go up to people in church on a Sunday morning and ask them if they know Jesus, I would get a positive response from most everybody. Everybody knows who Jesus is.

That's not the issue. Because it's one thing to know about someone, and it's another thing to *experience* a person intimately.

The apostle Paul writes, "Yet indeed I also count all things loss for the excellence of the knowledge of Christ Jesus my Lord, for whom I have suffered the loss of all things, and count them as rubbish, that I may gain Christ" (Philippians 3:8).

To know Christ on a personal basis does not come naturally or without cost. Knowing about Christ is one thing, but knowing Him personally is quite a different thing. That was certainly Paul's experience before he became a Christ follower.

As a Pharisee, he knew all there was to know about the Messiah from the Old Testament. But it was on a journey to Damascus—a trip to further persecute the church—that Saul (Paul's name at the time) encountered the real Christ.

> Saul . . . went to the high priest and asked letters from him to the synagogues of Damascus, so that if he found any who were of the Way, whether men or women, he might bring them bound to Jerusalem. As he journeyed he came near Damascus, and suddenly a light shone around him from heaven. Then he fell to the ground, and heard a voice saying to him, "Saul, Saul, why are you persecuting Me?"
>
> Acts 9:1–4

It was at this moment that Saul transformed into the Paul we know of today.

Following this Damascus transformational moment, Paul went into the desert for approximately three years. I believe he was unlearning religion during those years in order to understand who Jesus Christ really is.

Moses spent forty years in the wilderness to unlearn Egypt so God could use him to lead His people into the promised land.

Jacob was another Old Testament character who had such a transformation: "Then Jacob awoke from his sleep and said, 'Surely the LORD is in this place, and I did not know it'" (Genesis 28:16).

The Lord was with Jacob all the time, and he did not know it. His life changed when he encountered the Lord.

With the apostle Paul, it was the same. During his desert journey, Paul experienced Christ in a way that transformed him so completely that God was able to use him to lead like Christ and establish the church of Christ as we have it today.

The foundation of my spiritual ministry is to personally know Christ in such a way that my life has been transformed. To do this, I have needed to unlearn the world and be filled with the Holy Spirit.

To lead like Christ, we need to work in resurrection power that has nothing whatsoever to do with the world's elements. I can't emphasize it enough: This begins with a transformational encounter with Jesus Christ. Out of this experience will flow a passion and desire to serve Christ that colleges and seminaries cannot provide.

I like Charles Spurgeon and the requirement they had at Pastor's College. They would not accept an applicant for the college until he could prove he had been called of God for ministry. Spurgeon's idea was that you don't go to college to discover your call. You go to college because you have been called of God to serve.

This perspective is lacking today. Consequently, our churches are suffering drastically because of the lack of Christ-led leadership.

My purpose is to inspire you to discover your calling in Christ that will enable you to receive the power and the anointing of the Holy Spirit in your life. As you build on the spiritual foundation of Christ, you will begin to see ministry from a completely different perspective. You will see ministry as Christ sees it and see people as Christ sees them.

I praise You, O Father, for the love You show to all of us in allowing us to be part of Your work here on earth. Help me today to surrender to Your way of doing ministry that I would honor You. I ask this in Jesus' name. Amen.

2

Lead like Christ
THE MODEL

To Titus, a true son in our common faith: Grace, mercy, and peace from God the Father and the Lord Jesus Christ our Savior.

Titus 1:4

As stated earlier, this book is based on Paul's letter to Titus. Because of that, I need to share a short biography of Titus—Paul's example of what a Christ-led servant should be.

The poet Alexander Pope once said, "The proper study of mankind is man."[1] This is true because people take more interest in people than in ideas. I find it hard to get people interested in abstract ideas, but not in people. When you find a person who is the incarnation of a great idea, then you have a jewel indeed, a treasure. In both Paul and Titus, we have this jewel. In the man Paul, we have the incarnation of the doctrine he preached. And Titus, Paul's spiritual son in a way, is an incarnation of the great doctrines of the New Testament.

To Be a Christ-Led Servant

There are several things about this man, Titus, that I need to lay out if we are to understand what it means to be a Christ-led servant. We will first look at Titus the man.

Titus was not a Jew, but an uncircumcised Greek with a Roman name. In many ways, he was a big man, not so much in size but rather in influence. He was a native of Antioch in Asia Minor, where there was a healthy Christian

1. Alexander Pope, "An Essay on Man: Epistle II," https://www.poetryfoundation.org/poems/44900/an-essay-on-man-epistle-ii.

church. In Acts 11, we see that Paul was not the founder of the Antioch church. Still, Paul visited the church and often preached there.

At the time, Christians were scattered abroad because of the persecution that followed when Stephen was martyred, and Antioch was one of those places. From Antioch, missionaries went to various locations. This was a healthy missionary church, and Titus was fortunate enough and blessed by God to be born in that city.

I suppose Titus, in his early life, had been a believer in some kind of god. The Romans came in some years before and spread around their ideas of the gods. There was Zeus, the main Greek god, and Jupiter, his counterpart, the main Roman god. There were many others, and no doubt, this man Titus was a religious man. Enough so, when he listened to the message of Christ, it changed his life. He, presumably, had lots of talents and abilities.

Then we come to Titus the Christian.

When Titus came in contact with Paul, that blazing apostle, he surely was eternally thankful. Indeed, the whole church of Christ should be forever grateful that these two giants met. When this pagan man with a Roman name and Greek genealogy met this man Paul with a Hebrew background, now converted to Jesus Christ, Titus's conversion was clear, revolutionary, and instant.

Now we look at Titus, the assistant to the apostle.

Paul was not an easy person to please, and probably not easy to work with. Not because he was churlish or had a bad temper. He was not and did not. No, Paul was a sanctified man. He expected everybody to be just as devoted as he was and expected them to bid good-bye to the world, burn their bridges behind them, destroy their old life, and live in the new. If they did not, he undoubtedly was disappointed.

Although hard to please, Paul trusted Titus completely and used him as his representative. When Paul could not journey somewhere, he would send Titus. When he could not stay in a certain place, he would leave Titus. Their relationship is a beautiful example of the unity in Christ.

The old Pharisee Paul, who once wore his long robe and stood at corners uttering long prayers, was self-righteous to the point of keeping his nose in the air like an old codger looking down on others. But God met Paul on the Damascus road and completely transformed him, filled him with the Holy Ghost, gave back his eyesight, and eventually made him fall in brotherly love with the young Gentile, Titus. Pharisee Paul would not have shaken hands with that Gentile before his conversion. Now he called Titus "my son," gave him heavy responsibility, and loved him. That is what the grace of God will do for people.

Then we have Titus the missionary.

Titus traveled with Paul to Macedonia and Corinth and Crete.

Today, missionaries often spend years learning other languages in order to reach people. But Paul and Titus traveled around preaching in Greek, and almost everybody understood them. So it was relatively easy for them to travel as missionaries, as far as language was concerned.

Then there was Titus the man who did good.

It is said of Christ in Acts 10:38 that He was anointed with the power of the Holy Ghost and went about doing good. Here was Titus, following in Christ's steps, going about doing good for the poor saints of Jerusalem who needed help at the time.

Jerusalem was where the gospel got its start and where Christ was crucified. It was where the Holy Ghost fell on the apostles and was the center out of which their message spread.

Paul loved Jerusalem and became interested in taking an offering for the Jewish saints there. And where do you suppose this Jew went to get that offering? Gentile Christians.

> Moreover, brethren, we make known to you the grace of God bestowed on the churches of Macedonia: that in a great trial of affliction the abundance of their joy and their deep poverty abounded in the riches of their liberality. For I bear witness that according to their ability, yes, and beyond their ability, they were freely willing, imploring us with much urgency that we would receive the gift and the fellowship of the ministering to the saints.
>
> 2 Corinthians 8:1–4

Paul desired that Titus also would join his efforts. Paul wrote, "But thanks be to God who puts the same earnest care for you into the heart of Titus. For he not only accepted the exhortation, but being more diligent, he went to you of his own accord" (2 Corinthians 8:16–17).

Corinth was a well-to-do church, while Jerusalem was in need. But Titus had a plan. *I'm going to kill two birds with one stone. I'll kill poverty in Jerusalem, and I'll kill stinginess in Corinth.*

Titus went to the Corinthian church and essentially said, "I've come to give you an opportunity to do something wonderful."

"What's that, Brother Titus?" they responded.

"Well," he said, "I've come to allow you to give an offering for the poor saints in Jerusalem."

I can imagine some old deacon might have stood up and said, "Now, just a minute, Titus. We're Gentiles, and those people in Jerusalem think we're dirt. They wouldn't have anything to do with us."

With his Christlike attitude, Titus replied, "You don't know them. They're Jews, but they're Christians and have changed their attitude against us Gentiles. Besides that, they're hungry. What difference does it make what they think of you? The question is, What are you going to do for them?"

And with that, of his own accord, Titus took an offering from Corinth. That was the man Titus.

Always expect more from people who have more.

Then there was Titus the organizer.

When Paul sent Titus to Corinth to help straighten out that church, he explained, "For this reason I left you in Crete, that you should set in order the things that are lacking, and appoint elders in every city as I commanded you" (Titus 1:5).

In Titus was a remarkable union of enthusiasm, integrity, and discretion.

God gives different gifts to different men, and to Titus, He gave the gift of organizing. Titus could walk right into a disorganized, bumbling church and pull it back to order.

Finally, there was Titus the optimist.

In general, I do not like the word *optimism*. Crackpot poets have used the word in the wrong way. However, Titus was a cheerful brother, valued by Paul: "I had no rest in my spirit, because I did not find Titus my brother" (2 Corinthians 2:13).

Paul was an apostle and probably one of the half dozen great intellects of all time. Indeed, he is the greatest theologian the church ever produced. He had all these gifts yet was subject to despair and needed someone to come along and say, "Paul, God is still on the throne."

Imagine that old Pharisee needing the consolation and a good cheerful talk from a Gentile years younger than him. That is a gift in itself, to be able to console an apostle.

Titus had that. In Titus was a remarkable union of enthusiasm, integrity, and discretion. Those are three beautiful words.

A Beautiful Reflection of Christ

First, there is enthusiasm. I like enthusiasm. Most Christians drag their feet. Half the work of the preacher is to get people to lift their feet and stop dragging.

Many Christians, when it comes to the work of the Lord, have to be dragged, pushed, or pulled up, but not Titus. Titus was enthusiastic; he came out of the prayer room enthusiastic and had integrity. He was a sound man.

I pray that God would give us this kind of spirituality so we can pour ourselves out as Titus did.

When Paul wanted to appoint someone to carry that offering amounting to a lot of money to Jerusalem, you know who he appointed? Titus. Titus could be the treasurer, and you would not even have to audit his books. Titus went back to the Gentiles and carried to Jerusalem the gifts of the Macedonians and Corinthians and other churches, so he had enthusiasm linked with integrity.

Along with that came discretion. Some of the Lord's dearest people are good, honest people but not discreet. They say and do the wildest things, but not Titus. Paul trusted

Titus because he had discretion and integrity linked with enthusiasm.

I pray that God would give us this kind of spirituality so we can indeed be the Christians of the first order and pour ourselves out as Titus did.

God honors us by using us and working through us. He gives us a missionary mind and teaches us to give our goods to feed the hungry. A person truly does God's work by giving to missions or a church or by giving a little gift to somebody. This keep us optimistic and enthusiastic.

This is a brief picture of this man Titus, who, according to the apostle Paul, was a beautiful reflection of the Lord Jesus Christ.

This was Paul's idea of leading like Christ and the pattern Paul has for us today. The rest of this book, built on Paul's estimate of Titus, lays down the foundation of what spiritual leadership must look like.

O heavenly Father, I praise You for men like Paul and Titus. I pray that You would raise up men like that in our day. Challenge me, O God, to walk in ministry as they walked to the honor and glory of God. Amen.

3

Lead like Christ

A DEMONSTRATION

Paul, a bondservant of God and an apostle of Jesus Christ, according to the faith of God's elect and the acknowledgment of the truth which accords with godliness.

Titus 1:1

One problem facing the evangelical church today is that we believe we can create our own model of ministry—a model not based on Scripture but from the culture around us. If I am to lead like Christ, I need to demonstrate in my daily life a complete surrender to Christ, knowing that surrender will cost me everything.

Paul introduces himself to Titus as a servant of God, but Paul is not only a servant of Christ, he is a servant for a purpose. "I'm an apostle," Paul said, "and I'm a sent one." He served the Lord Jesus as the messenger to bring God's elect to the knowledge of the truth.

To lead like Christ demands the heart of Christ. And here we have a demonstration of that heart. A heart that knows the future outcome and rises above human understanding.

In the first verse of Titus, Paul calls himself "a bond-servant of God and apostle of Jesus Christ, according to the faith of God's elect."

What about this "God's elect"? We frequently pass this phrase over. A Christ-led servant refuses to do that. *God's elect* means "a divine choice." The New Testament teaches the doctrine of election. I do not understand it fully. In that great day when the Lord gives us a body like unto His glorious body and a brain in keeping with our glorious body and a mind in keeping with our glorious brain, we will understand the doctrine of election or realize that we cannot understand it. The learned man is not necessarily a man who understands everything, but a man who understands he cannot understand it all.

There is a song we sing at camp meetings,

We'll Understand It Better By and By

By and by, when the morning comes,
when the saints of God are gathered home,
we'll tell the story how we've overcome,
for we'll understand it better by and by.

Charles Albert Tindley (1851–1933)

We may not understand what "elect" means, but two things we can understand. One is only the elect will come. For Jesus said, "No one can come to Me unless the Father who sent Me draws him; and I will raise him up at the last day" (John 6:44).

So only the elect will come, but anyone who will come can come.

D. L. Moody, who was not known as a theologian but had an unusual flair for little concise gems of theology, settled the whole election question like this. He said, "'The elect' are the 'whosoever will's': the 'non-elect' are the 'whosoever won'ts.'"[1] So you can go and give a bona fide message of truth to everybody in the world and say, "If you come you will be saved," and if they come, they will be saved.

I'm not sure how to say it any better. We get so caught up in our old limited definition of doctrine and divide ourselves. I do not believe there will be such division in heaven.

1. Dwight Lyman Moody, *Notes from My Bible: From Genesis to Revelation* (Chicago: Fleming H. Revell Company, 1895), 108.

I believe that we will all be together in Christ, and it is Paul's concern to demonstrate that kind of leadership in the church.

To Be Transformed and Purified

Paul says, "The truth which accords with godliness." This is the burning core of the message that God, through Paul, gives to Titus.

The gospel of Jesus Christ works not only to rescue us. It purifies and transforms. We have emphasized the rescue part in recent years. Everybody says the same, "Come and be rescued." But the Bible does not stop there.

The book of Titus teaches that the elect must live lives of holiness and godliness. Paul reminds Titus that all around him is the doctrine of the Cretans, who were mixing their understanding of God with their Greek gods and mythology. Cretans were liars. And in some ways, many Americans are the Cretans of today. And if you are not a converted Christian and do not have the grace of God in your heart, they will influence you.

In Paul's day, Christians were a minority surrounded by Cretans, and Paul said to look out for these Cretans and rebuke them sharply so that they might be sound in the faith and live the right kind of life.

The whole level of morality today is low. If you want to live for Christ, you are going to have to turn your back on all and say, "No, I'll go with Christians, I'll live with Christians. My people are Christian, and I walk not with the ungodly."

According to the New Testament, if there is not some degree of transformation and purification, there is no guarantee of salvation, no matter how many times you have renewed your consecration. No matter how many cards you have signed or how many revival meetings you have attended, and no matter how many times you have thought you were accepting Christ, if there is not a good degree of transformation and purification, there is no guarantee of salvation, for the salvation that truly saves also transforms and purifies. This is the essence of Paul's letter to Titus, that he might instruct these Cretans.

Could Crete be any worse than some of our cities today? Historians say Crete was a bad mixture of evil religions, but could it be any worse than what we see today?

Unfortunately, some people will not let you help them, including those who call themselves Christians but are not transformed. They think they have all they need. Paul is basically saying, "Get with the people of God, get into the prayer meetings and young people's meetings and church meetings. See to it that you allow yourself to be helped, because you can be sure of one thing: The Cretans are out to get you. They're after you everywhere, and if you refuse to be helped by the children of God, then you will be dragged down by the Cretans, which God forbids."

A Focus on Purpose

Paul, as a servant of Christ, had a purpose and never allowed anything to compromise that purpose. He was an amazing model for this young Christian called Titus. It is not enough just to follow Christ; there is a purpose behind it all. Many do not know that purpose and flounder in their ministry and therefore compromise the work that God wants to do through them.

My greatest challenge is to discover God's purpose for my life. To find out why He is leading me one way and not the other. If I do not understand the purpose of serving God, I am going to be very confused concerning what God is doing in my life. Many Christians do not understand that what God is doing in their life is a reflection of the purpose He has put into them, which is to serve.

Paul served God for a purpose, rooted in who God was and how God had called him to be such a servant.

One thing we know for sure about the apostle Paul, and I believe it flowed over into the life of Titus, is that Paul never forgot his purpose. All the things that he endured and went through never took away his focus on purpose. He was serving God for a purpose, rooted in who God was and how God had called him to be such a servant.

I have discovered in my ministry that when I lose focus on my purpose, I am vulnerable to discouragement and even depression. The apostle Paul was human, and I believe he experienced such moments in his life. For me, the only thing that can lift me out of this cesspool is to get my focus back on my purpose in serving God.

I am sure that as Titus observed the apostle Paul, he discovered how to keep his own focus on God's purpose in his life.

Titus certainly demonstrated by his passion and actions what it looks like to lead like Christ. He demonstrated to the Christians of his day what it really means to follow Christ.

O Father, I praise You for models like Paul and Titus to encourage my life. Allow my life to be used of You in such a way that I do not lose the focus on my purpose in serving You. May all I do model complete dedication in living for and in serving You regardless of the cost. Amen.

4

Lead like Christ

MOTIVATED BY THE COMPLETE TRUTH

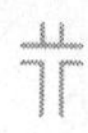

Paul, a bondservant of God and an apostle of Jesus Christ, according to the faith of God's elect and the acknowledgment of the truth which accords with godliness, in hope of eternal life which God, who cannot lie, promised before time began.

Titus 1:1–2

To lead like Christ, it is necessary to have the kind of motivation that led Christ. This motivation is not something we imagine or create or bring in from the outside culture. The motivation comes from its original source—the truth as it is in Jesus Christ.

To understand truth is a great challenge. For example, understanding the truth about eternal life is probably the greatest challenge. We need to get together all of the truth for it to be the real truth. That is our real hope.

I do not think anybody would even attempt to argue that eternal life is not a supreme treasure, for it is.

May we not overlook how valuable, how precious it is, or what a supreme treasure lies in those words *eternal life*. This is the life lost in the disobedience and the fall, yet brought again to us by the coming of Christ, who declared, "I have come that they may have life, and that they may have it more abundantly" (John 10:10). And everybody knows John 3:16: "For God so loved the world that He gave His only begotten Son, that whoever believes in Him should not perish but have everlasting life." Therefore, this supreme treasure lost once to us is now brought back to us by Jesus Christ and given by faith.

Finding the Synthesis

A question may arise when Paul says, "In hope of eternal life"; is that *hope* a future thing?

I think this so plain that it does not need to be labored. You hope for what you do not have. You cannot hope for what you already possess. Hope is lost in realization. Therefore, "in hope of eternal life" means that eternal life is future to the church.

So is eternal life present or future? Do we have it now, or are we looking for it? Again, the fact that Paul says "in the hope of eternal life" indicates that we are watching and hoping for it. If we had it, why would we yet hope for it?

Before we look further at what eternal life means, we need to explore a seeming contradiction of terms. People question why *eternal* and *everlasting* are used in different places in Scripture to modify the word *life*. Do they have different meanings?

There is such a thing as musical language—using certain words that are pleasing to the ear. This is why translators in one verse say "eternal life" and in another verse say "everlasting life." There would be places where "eternal life" would not fit in musically, so they changed it to "everlasting," since *everlasting* and *eternal* mean the same thing in Greek and are synonymous in English. If we say "eternal" or "everlasting" life, there is no difference. They are the same words from the lips of Jesus or from the pen of Paul or John.

Ralph Waldo Emerson once said, "A foolish consistency is the hobgoblin of little minds, adored by little statesmen and philosophers and divines."[1] Being in bondage to one line of thought is not scriptural because the truth is so vast and so many-faceted that it can rarely be stated in one proposition.

1. Ralph Waldo Emerson in John Bartlett, comp., *Familiar Quotations*, 10th ed., rev. by Nathan Haskell Dole (Boston: Little, Brown, 1919), Bartleby.com, 2000, https://www.bartleby.com/100/420.47.html.

That is precisely why the devil said, "It is written," and Jesus replied, "it is written." If Jesus had listened to the devil's "it is written," and if Jesus had been a textualist, He would have turned all those stones to bread and jumped off the tower. Had He been in bondage to words as some brethren are, He would undoubtedly have played straight into the devil's hands for fear of contradicting himself. But the fact is, truth is so vast that it can rarely be stated in a single proposition, and a single proposition usually is false in that it overstates the thing.

Remember that truth is a declaration plus what seems like a contrary declaration, then a getting together of the two. In philosophy, they call it a thesis, antithesis, and synthesis. Those are hard words when you lisp, but a thesis is something that you state. An antithesis is something contrary to that. And the synthesis is the combination of the two together, and that is where the truth lies.

Our problem is that we get ahold of a piece of truth and consider that truth to be all there is. We close our minds and then turn our backs on anybody that says anything different.

One man says, "I believe in God's sovereignty," so he closes his mind and welds it shut and believes in God's sovereignty. Another man stands up boldly and says, "I believe in man's free will," and closes the circle and welds it shut. The two men turn their backs on each other, walk away, and build two churches dedicated to their little circles. But the wise Christian takes thesis, antithesis, and synthesis, and says, "Now, just a minute. Is it possible that we can take both of these truths and see that they're both right and get to the third truth that's bigger than both of them?"

It is difficult to get people to do that. We would rather divide ourselves and build churches and be known as founders of something.

Let me present two propositions from Scripture about eternal or everlasting life that seem to contradict each other.

John 5:24: "He who hears My word and believes in Him who sent Me has everlasting life." Notice "has everlasting life" in the present tense.

And John 6:47 says, "Most assuredly, I say to you, he who believes in Me has everlasting life."

First John 5:12 says, "He who has the Son has life."

Three verses of Scripture establish the thesis that eternal life is the *present* possession of all true Christians. There we have a proposition with the approved text. The true Christian has eternal life.

We do not have to explain those verses. But some church people teach that eternal life is future, not to be possessed now. You will have it in the future, they say. Shall we close the ring and reject everybody that teaches anything but this? We have one thesis: Eternal life is the present possession of Christians.

But notice these passages:

Matthew 25:46: "And these will go away into everlasting punishment, but the righteous into eternal life." That is the future.

And Luke 20:35–36: "But those who are counted worthy to attain that age, and the resurrection from the dead, neither marry nor are given in marriage; nor can they die anymore, for they are equal to the angels and are sons of God, being sons of the resurrection."

There is a life, which is future, and it is something we are to obtain in the day ahead. Luke 18:29–30: "So He said to them, 'Assuredly, I say to you, there is no one who has left house or parents or brothers or wife or children, for the sake of the kingdom of God, who shall not receive many times more in this present time, and in the age to come eternal life.'"

Romans 2:7: "Eternal life to those who by patient continuance in doing good seek for glory, honor, and immortality."

Galatians 6:8: "For he who sows to his flesh will of the flesh reap corruption, but he who sows to the Spirit will of the Spirit reap everlasting life."

These and other verses establish the proposition that eternal life is the future possession of the Christian. So there we have a thesis and a contrary thesis.

What do we do? Throw up our hands and say the Bible contradicts itself? Should we say, "I do not know what to believe. I do not know what church to join," and just give it all up? Should we say that Christianity is such a confusion that we know nothing to do but go out and eat, drink, and be merry for tomorrow we die (1 Corinthians 15:32)?

That is the way of foolish people. There is another thing we can do. We can study these issues and see that instead of contradicting each other, they complement, supplement, and explain each other.

The thesis is that the Christian has eternal life now. The contrary thesis is that the Christian lives in the hope of eternal life. The synthesis, which is the truth, is that eternal life is to experience God in the soul. "And this is eternal life, that they may know You, the only true God, and Jesus Christ whom You have sent" (John 17:3). Therefore, eternal life is a present possession. It grows here in the bosom of redeemed men surrounded by death everywhere, for the world is asleep in the lap of wickedness and all is death around us. The Bible tells us that men are dead in trespasses and sins and they lie in the depth of iniquity and wickedness and bondage.

Amid all this mortality, death, bondage, and wickedness, some have eternal life now as a possession, for it is to know God and to know His Son Jesus Christ. Further, eternal life is also a future state. It is the kingdom of the blessed, and it is where death is banished forever. It is where the triune God is visibly present. It is where men shall look on the face of God, with no death present, and without the graveyards and the bones and the mortuaries and the undertakers and the hospitals and ambulances and the doctors and pain and woe in old age and death. Look upon the face of God of whom it is written, "Who alone has immortality, dwelling in unapproachable light, whom no man has seen or can see, to whom be honor and everlasting power. Amen" (1 Timothy 6:16). That is an expansion of eternal life.

Now we have, as it were, the little diamond of eternal life set in our heart, and ahead we shall dwell in mansions of diamonds.

Now we have, as it were, the little diamond of eternal life set in our heart, and ahead we shall dwell in mansions of diamonds. Now we have a little bit of the blue sky of eternal life to gaze upon like a prisoner looking at the blue sky through a narrow window. Ahead, there will be so much of it. We will be surrounded by eternal life. We will swim in it and fly in it and live in it.

God's Word Is Consistent

So you see, the Bible does not contradict itself. It merely states a proposition and then states another proposition, and it gives us credit for having the sense to say, "I believe this," or

"I believe that." The most pitiful thing I know is to see two saints sitting on the same log with their backs to each other who will not converse. One says eternal life is now, and the other one talks only about the hope of eternal life. If they would just get off that log and get a little perspective, they would see that both of those facts are true. A Christian has eternal life now, but he does not have all the eternal life there is now. He has God's life in his soul, for Peter says that we have the very nature of God in our souls now.

When you hear a man in a downtown mission tell a poor fellow from skid row, "Believe in Jesus Christ, and you have eternal life," he is telling the truth. When you hear the serious Bible expositor say, "We are living in the hope of eternal life to come," he is telling the truth too. Only what they mean is that the believer gets eternal life now. Paul calls it a foretaste, and that foretaste, which we have now, is just the beginning.

Now, when I say, "I have eternal life, thank God," and in the next breath I say, "The gospel is the hope of eternal life," people say, "There he goes again. We can't understand the man; he contradicts himself."

No, there's no contradiction there. God has given us now a little piece of what we are to have, but the great glorious inheritance waits for us there. So that is why the Bible often talks about looking for eternal life and hoping unto eternal life. The righteous go away into eternal life, but eternal life is in the righteous now.

When the Lord lays down a fact, believe that fact. When the Lord lays down another fact that seems to contradict it, believe that fact, for they are both true, and in a short time you will see a third truth that will show how they both fit into each other.

We Christians have eternal life now; that is the thesis. We look forward to eternal life, and that is the contrary thesis, but the synthesis is that eternal life has two meanings. It has the meaning of what we have now, and it has the meaning of what we are going to have. If any Christian thinks what they have now is all God can do for us, they will have to rethink this whole deal. The happiest and holiest Christian that ever lived is only a beginner, and he is just in kindergarten now—he is just playing on the shore with a sand bucket. There is yet an ocean lying before him, an ocean of glorious truth, of riches, which Christ has ready for him yonder.

Unless we pull all the truth together, we will not be able to exercise the leadership that Jesus Christ modeled for us when He was here on earth.

Deep is calling unto deep at the noise of God's waterspouts, and one of these times, all the little lagoons we call Christians, little puddles of eternal life, so to speak, will just suddenly burst over their dikes and rush out to meet that great vast ocean of eternal life, of which we call God. That is what we hope for, so Paul says, "Unto the hope of eternal life."

Unless we pull all the truth together, we will not be able to exercise the leadership that Jesus Christ modeled for us when He was here on earth. It is all the truth, or it is none of the truth.

Heavenly Father, I sincerely surrender to Your truth, which is the only truth worth surrendering to. Help me, O God, not to be sidelined by anything that compromises the whole truth. Use me, O Father, to live the truth of Christ in such a way that people will see the truth. Amen.

5

Lead like Christ

THE FRAMEWORK OF GOD'S PROMISES

In hope of eternal life which God, who cannot lie, promised before time began.

Titus 1:2

Building Christlike leadership qualities within us and others requires understanding God's promises. We need to know what the promises are and how they pertain to us and the people we're trying to serve.

In our study of Titus, we come to another important part of the text: "God, who cannot lie, promised before time began." We know, of course, that *God* here is the God of Abraham, Isaac, and Jacob—the God and Father of our Lord Jesus Christ, whom Paul said to be the only God. We have one Father, one God, and the hope of eternal life in the broader aspects of the world to come.

A promise is only as sound as the one who makes it. Look into who made the promise, and if the initial report is satisfactory, you have some sense of its reliability. Then, further investigate the record of the promise giver, whether he or she is 100 percent sound and has always come through on their promises. If the person has never been known to be anything but honest and true—if they can make good on the promise—there's no need to worry.

Say you get a letter promising you something. You might be skeptical, but still, you hope the promise is real. You may even ask God, "Father, help me to believe."

If I got such a letter and found it was simply a kind promise by a man who hadn't always come through, I would smile it off. But if I knew the man had kept past promises and was capable of keeping this one, I would trust his word.

This is how it is with the promises of God. He cannot lie. All truth begins with and rests upon Him.

It is painful to see people struggle to have faith—to believe in God and His promises. They have detached the promise from who made it. When God makes a promise, He can be trusted.

Knowing God in the Negative

It is interesting that Paul, here in Titus 1:2, speaks about God in the negative—that He *cannot* lie.

Thomas Aquinas, in his book *Of God and His Creatures*, expressed that we can know God more perfectly from negative statements about His character than from affirmative ones. God's nature is so infinitely removed from ours that we, fallen men and women, find it difficult to describe God. Thus, we can know what God *is not* better than we can know what God *is*. Theologians take a similar approach. To understand God's perfections, they often speak of negatives.

All truth begins with and rests upon God.

For instance, if I were to teach on God's self-evidence, I would say, "God had no origin." I do not know how else to express it, because human language is limited. Everything else had an origin, including the very seraphim and archangels. But God had no origin, so He must exist in himself, and thus we get the positive using the negative.

If I were to teach or meditate on God's self-sufficiency, I would say, "God has no support." And if God has no support, He must hold himself up. Therefore, He must be self-sufficient. So, by a negative, we arrive at a positive.

If I were to meditate on God's immutability, I would say, "God knows no change." If God does not change, He must always have been what He is now. Therefore, it is easy to reason that He will always be what He was and is.

If I were to meditate on God's infinitude, I would say, "God has no limitations." If God has no limitations, it can only mean that He is boundless and limitless.

Numerous passages in Scripture describe God by what He is not:

> The Lord "neither faints nor is weary." (Isaiah 40:28)
> "For I am the LORD, I do not change." (Malachi 3:6)
> "He who keeps you will not slumber." (Psalm 121:3)
> "He cannot deny Himself." (2 Timothy 2:13)
> "With God nothing will be impossible." (Luke 1:37)
> "It is impossible for God to lie." (Hebrews 6:18)

Paul used a negative statement when he said, "God, who cannot lie." If he had simply said "the true God" or "the God of truth," we could have figured it out all right. But it is more powerful when presented negatively.

God cannot lie. He gave us the promise of eternal life. What are you going to do? Go home, sweat it out, wonder if it is true? No. Get acquainted with God and be at peace. Acquaint yourself with Him, and you will not worry.

To Whom God Promises

Paul says God promised before time began. If He promised before time began, He must have promised to somebody present, and if He promised before the eternal ages, He must have promised to somebody who was before the ages were.

Now then, to whom was the promise made?

I once read a sermon of John Flavel, an old Puritan-type preacher, on the text from Isaiah 53:12 (KJV): "Therefore will I divide him a portion with the great, and he shall divide the spoil with the strong." Flavel said this indicated the Father made a covenant with the Son before the world was and before man was, and that covenant rested not upon man, but upon God. Man's salvation was a contract made between the Father and the Son.

Our certain hope for the future rests upon this God. Not on anything we see, touch, taste, or smell. Not on politics, civilization, financial conditions, or all the rest.

Christianity rests upon God and predates not only all political systems but also all people. It goes back before eternal ages and links itself like a mighty chain to the mighty throne of God. Some say political systems can stand alongside Christianity, but I do not believe it for a moment. Politics do not change our hope of eternal life.

God does nothing He has not covenanted to do with His eternal Son before an angel wing trembled by the sea of fire.

Others say Christianity goes along with all of civilization. Yet, civilization could go back to the oxcart or even disappear, and it would not change anything in heaven yonder. Civilization will not change the covenants of God or the God himself who promised His Son in a holy contract before the ages began. He will not fail us if our sub-civilization is destroyed.

"God never does anything new," said Meister Eckhart, and by that, he meant that God never does anything suddenly or impulsively. God says in Scripture, "Behold, I will do a new thing. . . . I make all things new" (Isaiah 43:19; Revelation 21:5), but He is talking about *our* new. He only talks from our side. In essence, God tells us, "Behold, I will do something that *to you* will seem new." He does nothing He has not covenanted to do with His eternal Son before an angel wing trembled by the sea of fire.

If God blesses you today, if He answers your prayer, He promised it before time. If He saves you today, He does it according to a covenant He made with His Son before the eternal ages. So God never does anything new.

When God made His will, He sealed it in blood and settled it. The God who cannot lie swore by himself because He could swear by no other. Our inheritance is in Him.

> [God] has saved us and called us with a holy calling, not according to our works, but according to His own purpose and grace which was given to us in Christ Jesus before time began.
>
> 2 Timothy 1:9

> In Him we have redemption through His blood, the forgiveness of sins, according to the riches of His grace which He made to abound toward us in all wisdom and prudence, having made known to us the mystery of His will, according to His good pleasure which He purposed in Himself, that in the dispensation of the fullness of the times He might gather together in one all things in Christ, both which are in heaven and which are on earth—in Him. In Him also we have obtained an inheritance, being predestined according

> to the purpose of Him who works all things according to the counsel of His will, that we who first trusted in Christ should be to the praise of His glory.
>
> Ephesians 1:7–12

Do not worry about these promises, nor about the God who made them. Instead, concern yourself with loving Him as you should and living as you should, being useful and truthful as God wants you to be.

Never insult the Majesty in the heavens by doubting Him, for He is the God who cannot lie, the God who promised eternal life before time began. And we who believe in Him are now part of that eternal contract He made with His Son before the eternal ages.

O God, I trust You as I trust nobody else. Much concerning Your promises is beyond my understanding but not beyond my accepting. With all that is within me, I accept Your promises, and with Your grace, I will live according to them from now to eternity. Amen.

6

Lead like Christ

MANIFESTED THROUGH PREACHING

[God] has in due time manifested His word through preaching, which was committed to me according to the commandment of God our Savior.

Titus 1:3

Spiritual leadership depends a great amount on the ministry of preaching.

Preaching is not an art, as many think. Books can teach you how to be the best preacher you can be. There's nothing tragically wrong with that, but I would rather be a poor preacher imitating the leadership of Christ in my sermons than be the planet's best preacher. The question becomes, Am I preaching to impress, or am I preaching in such a way that Christ is flowing through me to the people I'm ministering to?

As we study Titus, observe that Paul could have put a period after "has in due time manifested His word." But he did not. He added a little prepositional phrase, "through preaching," demonstrating that Paul's preaching was committed to Paul according to the command of God our Savior.

I do not think in all my years I have ever felt weight quite like those two words: *through preaching*. I think of God's condescension that He should use these words at all. How remarkably sure of himself God must be to entrust such a perfect plan to such an imperfect medium. This perfect plan of God, drawn up between the persons of the Godhead before time, was a plan to recover man from his lost condition, to reclaim him after his fall and reinstate him after his disgraceful expulsion, to give him eternal life and at last immortality.

The laws of God being what they are, God being who He is, and His nature being what it is, this was not easy. This plan had to do with the morality and the structure of the universe. It had to do with the very foundations upon which rest the heavens, the earth, and all things visible and invisible. And God had to work out a plan to lay creation's blueprints, then build according to those blueprints, and then unveil the structure. It took God to do that, and He did it in a manner infinitely perfect and excellent—as might be expected of a God beyond the power of language to describe.

That is the perfection of the plan, and now, wonder of wonders, God makes this known through preaching, one of the most imperfect of mediums. Why is preaching imperfect? Because language is involved, and wherever language is involved, there is imperfection.

Language does become profound when it deals with religion and the soul of a man. Still, there is always imperfection, for the simple reason that language is fluid and changes. Because of the many languages all over the world, our missionaries tell us rather heartbreaking and humorous stories of their effort to get ideas across. Even nations that use the same language use different words to mean the same thing. Language also tends to localize itself, so a particular word does not mean the same thing in another locality. A simple example: We get into an elevator in America and into a lift in England.

Imperfect Leaders, Yet Used by God

Then I think of the enormous crushing obligation resting upon leaders who stand to declare the truth anywhere. Messengers of the Most High God, they come clothed with the authority of the Most High God with a message from the Most High God. Yet no secret document ever carried in any portfolio by any ambassador, however top secret it might be, can compare with the seriousness and weight of the message carried by the simplest, poorest preacher that stands today, ready to preach to a little flock.

Yes, the future of millions lies in the hands of those that preach the Word and the teachers who stand before their classes to declare the Word. That is a form of preaching too. Do not rule that out—giving the Word, teaching the Word, instructing, exhorting, and inspiring men and women and young people.

I think of the man who got up lazy one morning, head aching, and said to himself, "I don't think I will pray today as much. I think I'll rest." So he puttered around the house, but before long, the Spirit of God began to move him, and he declared, "I gotta pray." As he prayed, the light of God came on him. Then he went out that night or the next Sunday and preached, and somebody was converted. The conversion of that person resulted in the conversion of one of your ancestors, resulting in the conversion of someone else in your family line, all the way down to you. You now are a Christian, and your home is Christian because somebody back then did not fail God.

No secret document ever carried by any ambassador can compare with the seriousness and weight of the message carried by the simplest, poorest preacher that stands today.

Ministry can be a very good place for a lazy man to indulge his talents, for nobody will check on him. He can sleep until noon, and if he gets a phone call at ten o'clock, he can get up and try to sound alert. But how can a man upon whose head God has laid His hands ever be lazy when you consider the condescension of God that He made His perfect plan through the imperfect medium of preaching? With the mighty obligation that lies in Christian leaders, how can they be lazy? How can they be careless? And yet, some are.

How could a man be cowardly when preaching a message God has given him? Yet there are preachers who back out on His message and on the truth, saying afterward, "I didn't mean to offend you." Preachers are not above apologies, of course. If he is a Christian man, he ought to apologize if he has hurt anybody, but he should never be afraid.

Then there is the covetous man, whom I do not understand. The man who allows the church board's offer of money to determine whether he will preach. Read what Ezekiel says: "Son of man, I have made you a watchman for the house of Israel" (Ezekiel 3:17). Think how terrible this is, yet we can dare to think holy thoughts and mingle them with money and popularity and what people think and say.

The Responsibility of Hearers

Then there is the overwhelming responsibility that rests upon the hearer. What puts the hearer under obligation? The source of the message, for one thing. Throughout Scripture, God states, "The Most High God, Son of Man, I said this . . ." and "Go tell them I said this . . ." and the like.

Even elementary things of the gospel put the hearer under obligation.

Remember, the sermon is not done when the benediction is pronounced. Nobody is finished taking in the message when the preacher says, "And lastly . . . amen." The hearer may sleep, and some do. The hearer may scorn, and some do. The hearer may resist, and some do. But all will certainly face their responsibilities on that great day.

Do we realize we are the children of eternity? Do we realize that we were born to die once down here? We will rise again in heaven or hell, and then face up to things.

God told Ezekiel, "If you warn the wicked, and he does not turn from his wickedness, nor from his wicked way, he shall die in his iniquity; but you have delivered your soul" (Ezekiel 3:19). Ezekiel knew how serious the charge of God is and that the wicked die in their iniquity.

God also told Ezekiel, "If you warn the righteous man that the righteous should not sin, and he does not sin, he shall surely live because he took warning; also you will have delivered your soul" (Ezekiel 3:21).

So there we have it—two sides of the same coin: a preacher with his obligation to tell and the hearer with his obligation to hear.

May God Have Mercy

I say, "God have mercy on us all." May God have mercy on preachers who fail. Mercy on that prophet called of God who thinks more of his home and his car and his salary and comfort than he does of the souls of men. God have mercy on that cowardly man who edits out the offensive things of the doctrine for fear that some hierarchy will review him or he will get a reputation for not being sound. Young people, let me encourage you, in particular. You can live down reputations that would kill some people. The Holy Ghost comes on you; you get blessed, you bless people, and demand increases for your preaching and leadership. Then those who were trying to stand in your way cannot stand in your way anymore, so they accept you, pat your back, and say, "Well, I don't see it quite like you do, but carry on."

God have mercy on preachers who fail. I think of the time we have wasted and the time we have misused. I consider, as a man called of God when I was seventeen years old, how much I have wasted and what a poor wretch of a preacher I am compared to what I could have been if I had obeyed God.

Finally, God, have mercy on the hearers who ignore their responsibility and refuse to be affected by Your gospel.

I praise You, O God, for Your Word manifested through preaching. Thankfully, Your Word is not based upon my skill in preaching alone, but rather the Holy Spirit working through my preaching. It is not my preaching but Your manifestation through the preaching that is significant. May my preaching reflect Your presence alone. Amen.

7

Lead like Christ

UNDERSTANDING BIBLICAL ORDER

To Titus, a true son in our common faith: Grace, mercy, and peace from God the Father and the Lord Jesus Christ our Savior. For this reason I [Paul] left you in Crete, that you should set in order the things that are lacking, and appoint elders in every city as I commanded you.

Titus 1:4–5

To maintain Christ's likeness in our leadership, we need to understand biblical order. During Christ's ministry, He never violated biblical order. Indeed, He laid the foundation for such order.

Paul outlines for us what that biblical order is and how we are to use it in maintaining Christlike leadership. We should not make up things as we go. We are to conform to what has already been established for us.

We must not labor over elementary or obvious truths, however. We must build on them.

The Scriptures state many obvious things, and I would say a large percentage, if not almost 100 percent, of false doctrines comes out of the inability to know what to do with the obvious. If you listen to a sermon and say to yourself, "I can't deny that it was true, but it didn't do me any good; it was dull," then the speaker was laboring the obvious. He explained that which needed no explanation and laboriously ran over ground already cultivated.

The writer of Hebrews warned about this when he essentially said, "Leave the foundational doctrines, the elementary teaching, and let us go on to perfection, the laying on of hands, and baptisms. Let's move on" (see 6:1–2). You do not make progress by teaching over and over what everybody already knows.

Common Faith

Early in his letter to Titus, Paul called him "a true son in our common faith." You might wonder what "common faith" means because *common* is not always seen as a positive word. Indeed, the word has many definitions.

We talk about common bread and describe seeing an everyday thing as "a common sight." Paul talked about common temptations (1 Corinthians 10:13), and after Jesus appeared before Pilate, He was led into a common hall (Matthew 27:27 KJV). In these uses, *common* means the opposite of excellent or unique. Yet Paul turned around and used *common* to describe the faith of the fathers. Why?

Here again, do not get lost in the obvious, because *common* can also mean "open to everybody" or "shared by a group."

In England and Wales, for example, rural communities have places called commons—land not belonging to anybody but belonging to everybody commonly. Walk down a street most anywhere, and you're on a common sidewalk; go to a park, and it is common for everybody. That is one meaning of the word *common*: open to everybody.

Jude 1:3 refers to "common salvation," meaning it is open to everybody, not restricted to a small group.

Another meaning of *common* is "shared by a group." Suppose a man and his wife have a baby, but a few months later, the boy dies. The parents can rightly say to each other, "We share a common grief." Nobody else has that same level of grief. If another child is born, the parents can say, "She is our common joy."

That is what Paul meant by "common faith"—faith shared by a group of people, but not everybody.

The Need for Organization

Paul continues his letter to Titus with, "For this reason I left you in Crete." Crete was one of five large Greek islands, the other four being Sicily, Corsica, Sardinia, and Cyprus. Paul wanted Titus to stay in Crete in order to appoint elders for the churches. Early church fathers sought leaders over other aspects of their ministry too. In this passage, the disciples turned to a congregation to find the best people possible to assist the widows.

> Then the twelve summoned the multitude of the disciples and said, "It is not desirable that we should leave the word of God and serve tables. Therefore, brethren, seek out from among you seven men of good reputation, full of the Holy Spirit and wisdom, whom we may appoint over this business."
>
> Acts 6:2–3

When only two or three gathered together in the name of the Lord, there was no reason for organization. But as soon as a multitude of believers arose, there had to be some organization, as 1 Peter 5:1–3 also revealed:

> The elders who are among you I exhort, I who am a fellow elder and a witness of the sufferings of Christ, and also a partaker of the glory that will be revealed: Shepherd the flock of God which is among you, serving as overseers, not by compulsion but willingly, not for dishonest gain but eagerly; nor as being lords over those entrusted to you, but being examples to the flock.

Any group of Christians that meets together has to have some organization to function. Otherwise, there will be no order, only chaos and wasted motion. The great proof of this lies in 1 Corinthians 12, where Paul likens the church to the body. Your brain has to tell your nerves what to tell your muscles, and your muscles have to cooperate with your joints, and everything has to work together. So the church of Christ, if it is going to work, must be organized.

An authentic New Testament church must consist of offices, authority, and obedience. We must be ready and willing as Christians to admit this, because that is what the Bible teaches. If a congregation is not organized, I cannot help but pity them.

Led by the Holy Spirit

Good men sometimes say things they should never say. The nineteenth-century British preacher Charles Spurgeon was once asked, "Mr. Spurgeon, have you ever been ordained?" He is said to have replied, "No, nobody's ever laid his empty hands on my empty head." Spurgeon rejected ordination, and as a result, laymanism took over the evangelical church. Yet, Scripture is clear about biblical order. Look again at Acts 6: The "seven men of good reputation" did not begin their work until the apostles had prayed, laid their hands on them, and ordained them to the ministry (vv. 3–6).

God gives no man dictatorial authority over the church. He gives him a position and certain spiritual authority there, which, if the church is a church of God, they will recognize. But he has no right to call all the shots, rule everybody's life, and dictate. Absolutely not.

Peter said elders should be serving as overseers, not "as being lords over those entrusted to you, but being examples to the flock" (1 Peter 5:3). They are to be shepherds to the flock, not sergeants that command the flock. There is a difference, and good leaders are those who lead us, not those who command us.

The pastor is not a hired man. He is one of the crowd—ordained of God to take certain leadership—and the flock follows him as he follows the Lord. Never think of him as a man to be hired and fired at the direction of some board member.

We desperately need the right kind of leadership. What we are getting now is not the leadership of the Holy Spirit. It is a town-hall method of leadership with all sorts of new schemes and methodology. The people of the church are God's sheep and should have a voice in selecting those who set things in order. But keep in mind that if the great God Almighty does not ordain a man, he is not an elder, no matter how often he may be elected.

To function, the church needs Christlike leadership, fellowship, cooperation, and order. It is wonderful to work together and have everybody willingly doing their part. Where the Spirit of God is, I doubt there is any likelihood of difficulty. That only happens when carnality gets in.

If the great God Almighty does not ordain a man, he is not an elder, no matter how often he may be elected.

Dr. Samuel Johnson, the eighteenth-century British writer, once made one of the wisest, most penetrating observations ever made by an uninspired man. As the story goes, he was sitting around with others in his literary club, discussing everything in heaven and on earth. There was never anything too high or too low for them to discuss. They did not sit around, make quips, and tell jokes the way men do today. They discussed learned things. Dr. Johnson settled it for me and for all time when he said, "Sirs, I have observed that it makes little difference what form of government prevails in a country. The people will be happy only if the ruler is just."

If we are going to honor Christ and lead like Christ, we need to understand this and commit ourselves to it no matter the cost.

I praise You, Lord Jesus, that You are the head of the church and in charge. Help me to surrender to Your authority as it works out in my personal ministry. Use me according to Your desires to accomplish Your work for all eternity. Amen.

8

Lead like Christ

THE OBVIOUS FRUIT

For a bishop must be blameless, as a steward of God.

Titus 1:7

The fruit of leading like Christ is a church that reflects the character and nature of Christ. To lead like Christ, we must discipline believers to showcase God's amazing grace in their lives.

The Christ-led church will never mirror the culture, but will always reflect the Lord Jesus Christ in all of His glory. Our success comes not by imitating the world, but rather by imitating Christ.

We find ourselves living hundreds of years from the beginning of the New Testament church. Much water has gone over the dam, and much wind has blown across the moor. Many strong dictatorial minds have impressed themselves upon the church during the centuries. Today, we have differing views about bishops, elders, and deacons. The New Testament is not very clear about all of this. It lays down principles but leaves the outworking of those principles to the church.

Paul calls bishops stewards of God and says they must be blameless. Blamelessness is not a virtue. It is a summation of other virtues. Paul first said bishops are to be blameless, and then he laid it out, "Here's what I mean by 'blameless.' . . . " That was Paul's method.

To Be Blameless

What does Paul mean when he says bishops must be blameless as God's stewards? Paul is speaking about anybody who holds an office in the church. And if it's true of them, it certainly ought to be true of every one of God's children. God has no double standard. He does not say, "You saints are supposed to be very poor," and we draw our priesthood from the saints. God wants all of His people to be holy, and anything said here about an elder should also apply to the newest convert, or as soon as he can develop and grow in spirituality. At least, the standard is there for him.

It doesn't matter what office you hold in the church; if you are in any way a leader within the church, all this and its moral connotation to every true Christian applies to you.

The first thing about this man mentioned is that he is to be the husband of one wife. He is to be monogamous, and not have several wives, as they did in many parts of the world then and as they do now in some places. Crete was a melting pot for every sort of nationality, philosophy, and religion, and getting rid of one wife and living with another was common and accepted. Paul essentially said, "We are introducing the standard of morals, higher than anything known in Crete." While he didn't press it, he put it down as a rule. Every leader in church affairs, no matter what he does, if he's before the public and the public takes him as an example, must understand that he owes it to God and to the faith and the people to be right in this particular aspect.

Paul then says elders are to keep a decent house. It says here, "Having faithful children not accused of dissipation or insubordination" (v. 6).

Some people have been so conscientious about this that if a prospective leader's family hasn't been converted, he is not able to serve in the church. That is not what this means. I can only make it out to mean that the man given a position in the church should not have a reputation of running a loose house with his children coming in at all hours, drinking and smoking and rioting. The Christian home should be a decent place to live, and if you can't get all the children born again, at least you can say to them, as I've said a hundred times to mine, "Remember, the rules of the home are set, so if you're staying under this roof, you will obey the rules. There are some things we don't do here." I believe that's what Paul had in mind here.

For instance, if an elder in the church has lost complete control of his family, though the man may be good and may have wept long hours in prayer over this, he ought not to be in the place of leadership, because people are likely to judge him by his house. In the King James, it says his children should be faithful and "not accused of riot or unruly." What goes on in the hearts of his children he cannot help. But he can help what goes on in his home. The man who hasn't got enough gumption to see to it that his home is right hasn't got enough of what it takes to be a church leader. It takes not only compassionate spirituality to be a leader in the church, but also the ability to say yes and no.

Humble and Able to Work with People

The third thing about spiritual leaders is that they should not be self-willed. That is, a leader is not a headstrong fellow who will have his way even if it busts up the whole church. There's no sense in that, absolutely none. Yet some consider themselves before anything else.

We had a word on the farm for such a man: We called him bullheaded. A bullheaded man has no place in the pulpit. In my mind, one of the most bullheaded men who ever lived was Martin Luther, but he had to get over that. He had to come to a place where he said, "Old Luther has died, and the Lord lives within." And though it was normal for Luther to be strongly self-willed, he had to humble himself and learn to work with people.

My entire ministry has been a self-contradictory affair. I have a temperament that wants to take orders from nobody—to get along with nobody. And yet I have a spiritual conviction that I ought to, and so I do. My old English father was so self-willed and so independent that when he left the farm and came to the city, he resented his boss until he died because the boss told him what to do. My father didn't want anybody pushing him around.

By temperament, that's also how I feel. But doctrine and the Spirit and the teaching of the Word tell me that I can't get my way all the time. I will be voted down sometimes, and my opinion sometimes will get slaughtered. The Lord does this to keep me humble.

And so, we are not to be self-willed. A self-willed Sunday school superintendent won't get along with his teachers; a self-willed teacher won't get along with his class; a self-willed deacon won't get along with anybody.

In verse 7 of this passage, Paul says a leader also should not be quick-tempered.

There is no excuse for a bad temper. Let nobody blame it on their family or culture. If you have a bad temper, consider it a blemish of character. Go to God, and deal with it. Pray it through; weep it through until God delivers you from it.

Now, a man of high temper cannot promptly be meek. He has to have his temper purified and consecrated so that what used to be a temper that would make him blow up becomes an inward strength of character that makes him love righteousness and hate iniquity. He is stronger for that. But when the devil is in it, he simply gets an evil temper, and an evil temper is always bad. There's no excuse for it. Nobody has any right to get elected to anything in any church if he's got a bad temper.

Verse 7 also says elders should not be given to wine. I don't think I need to press this point. This cannot be part of spiritual leadership. If drinking wine causes a brother to stumble, I need to drink no wine.

Leaders also should not be violent. The King James says a leader should not be a "striker." This is almost funny, at first glance, but remember who Paul's writing to, the Cretans, and evidently, the way some people got their way in Crete was to use their fists. That's actually what *striker* means. It has no similarity whatsoever to striking, like employees sometimes do. Again, what it means here is using your fist to strike a blow. Think of an old deacon trying to get somebody else to do what he's told, and he punches him to get him to obey. You don't have to cuff people around to get obedience. The church has other ways to preach obedience.

Money and Hospitality

In our Scripture passage, Paul also says elders should not be greedy for money. ("Not given to filthy lucre," in the King James.)

I can hear Paul when he uses that word *money*, kind of rolling it off his tongue. He never had any money. Money is one thing, and filthy money is another thing. Of course, *lucre* means gain, and filthy lucre means gain gotten filthily or gain that is loved unduly so it therefore becomes filthy. So money is filthy only when you have made it filthy by your attitude toward it. On the other hand, Paul writes elsewhere what to do with money: "On the first day of the week," he essentially said, "let everybody bring his money in, lay it up, and give it to God that it may be given to those in need" (see 1 Corinthians 16:2–3).

Qualified elders must also be hospitable. The church should be an example to neighborhoods around it. The church never ought to take on the complexion of the neighborhood. Never should the church take on the moral complexion of the age in which it lives. The church is morally separated from the age in which it lives as Jesus Christ was separated from Rome. The church should be a separated people, and all of us should be this kind of meek and gentle and quiet and kind and generous people so that the world around us should know what kind of people we are and the very darkness should make the star of our church shine that much brighter. We should have that kind of a church from the newest convert to the oldest and most honored elder. Nobody should live a life that anyone can point to and say, "I don't like the kind of life you're living."

Our leadership should always reflect the values of Christ in all we do.

If you use Christianity to cover up the way you live, what you need is a revival, and you need it quickly, and you need it badly. We ought to live such perfectly clean, open lives everywhere we go—on buses and trains, at work, everywhere—so that when we get into a religious conversation, we won't be afraid to share our testimony by the way we live.

Our leadership should always reflect the values of Christ in all we do, and we should disciple believers under our ministry to do likewise. To lead like Christ always focuses on Christ and ends in Christ.

O Father, I submit to the full-time rules and order that You make for my life and ministry. Let me never get caught up in anything that would in any way compromise the work You have called me to do. Amen.

9

Lead like Christ

ATTRIBUTES OF A SPIRITUAL LEADER

For a bishop must be blameless, as a steward of God, not self-willed, not quick-tempered, not given to wine, not violent, not greedy for money, but hospitable, a lover of what is good, sober-minded, just, holy, self-controlled.

Titus 1:7–8

Nothing is more important in our spiritual leadership than the qualifications that bring us in line with Jesus Christ. These qualifications do not come from the world. Many leaders are too educated by the world to concentrate on the spiritual ramifications of ministry. We do not need business credentials, but rather an overwhelming call of God upon our life that does not permit us to do anything else.

As we introduced in the previous chapter of this book, Paul is telling another man of God, Titus, the qualifications for church leadership. I ask you to notice one thing here, which is in glaring contrast to our usual way of judging things. Notice that *intellectual* qualifications are entirely missing. Verse 9 does talk about the ability to "exhort and convict those who contradict." That would assume a fair degree of intellectual power, but the qualifications here are not intellectual. They are not what we would call gifted men in the human way of looking at it.

Biblical Hospitality

Paul says a qualification for leaders in the church is to be hospitable. What does *hospitable* mean?

The custom in those days for missionaries and workers, like Paul and Silas and Barnabas, was to travel from place to place. Paul named many of the places in his letters. They traveled on a shoestring, practically. They were always under pressure, and there was never a red carpet rolled out for them. Somebody grabbed a gray rock instead of a red carpet and was ready to throw rocks at Paul and his companions.

So Christians opened their homes to these traveling preachers, and here is what hospitality means. This does not mean to invite your relatives in. That is something good to do, and it is just taken for granted. That is all right for your relatives to visit and exchange visits and have them come and go. According to Bible commentators and translators, *hospitality* seems to refer to how they did it then. Christians threw their homes open to the traveling preachers. John warned against throwing their homes open to the wrong kind of preachers. If you open your home to a false teacher, you have partaken of those evil deeds. You even contribute to his delinquency.

In verse 8, Paul defines a hospitable leader as "a lover of what is good." In the King James, it reads "a lover of good men."

Sometimes translators disagree if *good* or *evil* means an abstraction or personality. For instance, the Lord's Prayer says, "Deliver us from evil" (Matthew 6:13 KJV). Translators do not know whether *evil* is a noun or an adjective exactly. They do not know whether that should be "deliver us from the evil one" or "deliver us from evil." Either way, though, it does not matter. They don't know whether Paul said, "a lover of good men" or "a lover of good," but in either case, it simply means that man's one quality or qualification of work in the church should be that he loves good and naturally loves good people. The question is, Where is your affinity?

Where Is Your Affinity?

I do not ask where you spend time, because some people spend time ministering in places where everybody is evil. You cannot help that. However, where is your affinity? Where do you go when you are free to go where you would? And where do you feel at home? And what kind of people do you see?

If you seek out worldlings, people who prioritize worldly pleasures, that ought to be found out. One should not be accepted as a good Christian who finds himself at home among worldlings. Again, some work with and have to be present at the gatherings of people like this. You have to go, but you do not like it. You get away as soon as you can, and you do not partake of any evil deeds, but it is a part of your job. Therefore, it is not the question of where you have to go sometimes, but where do you feel at home? Where are you when at rest? Where is your kind of people?

Everybody on an official board in the church ought to qualify as a lover of good and a lover of good people. I cannot see how a church can hope to have God's blessing on it if it tolerates people in places of leadership who are not lovers of good people or who feel at home among lukewarm believers or worldlings.

Responsible

Going on, Paul says a leader should be sober minded, not flighty. In the King James, verse 8 uses the word *sober*, but I think it has nothing to do with liquor. Paul dealt with that when he said we are not to be lovers of wine. Here, *sober minded* means "not reckless, not irresponsible, and not excitable."

Pastors know gifted, good people who are yet irresponsible and cannot be trusted with leadership. These people seek freedom, but it is not freedom; it is irresponsibility. Christ says, "Take my yoke upon you," but they will not wear a yoke. You cannot say they are going to hell. They say they are not—they will go to heaven by God's grace, they insist. People like this are unbroken colts. They just will not wear any harness. They say that they do not believe they should because that is contrary to Paul's doctrine of liberty. Still, Paul was very careful to teach that we had all kinds of liberty; we must lay all the responsibility on ourselves, for Christ's sake and the church's sake. But some are not willing to do that. So they are irresponsible, reckless, and somewhat excitable and flighty. While you like them, you cannot trust them, and there are thousands of them in the churches.

Then Paul says Christ-led leaders must be holy. That is their relation to God and temperament. This is your relationship with yourself. There we have again that famous triangle to which I call attention so often: our relationship with God, with our fellow men, and with ourselves. Paul calls it sober, righteous, and godly further on in his epistle. Here he calls it just, holy, and temperate. The temperate man is a man in right relationship to himself. The holy man is in right relationship to God, and the just man is in right relationship to everyone.

You might say, "I haven't always been that way." Well, start now. You cannot even hope to go back and undo all you have done, but you can start now. I love that beautiful Scripture, "Behold, I make all things new" (Revelation 21:5). Begin here and begin now. When a man or woman turns to God, God will trust them as if they have never done anything wrong. God starts now. Now is the accepted time: God's *now*. So the just man is the man who is honest toward his fellow man, the holy man is right in his relationship to God, and the temperate man is right in his relationship to himself.

Hold Fast to Sound Doctrine

According to Paul, qualified leaders must hold "fast the faithful word" (1:9). We must remember that Paul was not a technical man. He would not crucify you on a technicality, but he also was not a careless man.

Today, we live in an age of creedless religion. We do not believe anything in particular, people say. We just love everybody and love the Lord and gather together around a simple place of worship and fellowship, all going the same direction.

But Paul said we must hold fast the faithful word of sound doctrine. Paul was a doctrinaire—do not forget it. He said love was everything, but he also made doctrine to be the direction love took, and out of doctrine sprang love. So the church leader has to be a man who holds fast to the faithful word—no loose ideas, no personal interpretations, just the faithful word. He does this so that he may by sound doctrine be able to exhort and convince the gainsayers. He has to be able to do two things: He has to expound and expose. He is an informed man who knows the Scriptures with the ability to expound and expose. Expound is the positive. Expose is the negative. *To expound* is to tell what the Scripture says. *To expose* is to show where teachers are wrong.

The church leader must have the faithful word and sound doctrine and follow what he has been taught in the Word of God.

For an example, go to Galatians, Colossians, or 1 John. These are some pretty sharp exposés showing people for what they were. A good leader has to be informed and then have the ability to expound the teaching to some degree and show what is wrong so that people do not end in the woods. Just as sure as you live, a church that gets careless about its doctrine will land in the same place the man will who gets careless about watching the signs if he's traveling across the country and ends up somewhere on a dead-end street. Sound doctrine is the clearly marked highway. While it is not everything, it leads to God, and it is so vastly important that it dare not be neglected.

So, the church leader must have the faithful word and sound doctrine and follow what he has been taught in the Word of God. He must also be able to expound it so others can get it and defend it so that the gainsayers and vain talkers will not upset the children of God.

The local church and its leadership are not like anything out in the world. Great universities that started as institutions to prepare future church leaders have slowly gravitated to worldly preparation.

To lead like Christ, we must carry about us the attributes of Christ that are reflected through our ministry.

I pray, O heavenly Father, that I represent to the world around me what a spiritual leader must. I accept the responsibility to live the kind of life that You require to do the work that You have ordained. Amen.

10

Lead like Christ

UNDERSTANDING THE THREEFOLD QUALIFICATION

Holding fast the faithful word as he has been taught, that he may be able, by sound doctrine, both to exhort and convict those who contradict.

Titus 1:9

The job of spiritual leadership is to bring the church into complete harmony with the nature of Christ. This is not an overnight endeavor. It takes a lot of time and energy, and only through the Holy Spirit's power is it accomplished.

In Titus 1:9, Paul introduces a threefold qualification of Christian leaders: to hold "fast the faithful word" in order to teach the teachable and correct the mistaken.

Christ, the apostles, and the church fathers held that there is a fountain out of which truth proceeds. Christ was not searching for truth; Christ himself is that truth.

I suppose there is scarcely anything a man may set himself to do or claim for himself that is more comforting to his carnal ego than to imagine himself as a searcher for truth. I have talked to many intelligent people who assured me they were seekers of truth.

Christ's apostles were not seekers of truth. Neither were the church fathers. They searched *in the truth* that they might know more of the truth. The idea that they were searching up and down the universe, throughout all the corridors of human thought, to locate the truth is a pagan concept and not biblical.

No such idea ever entered the minds of the apostles and the church fathers. They believed that there is a criterion against which all ideas are to be judged: absolute truth. Not, as some believe, relative truth.

Some truths here in this world are indeed pragmatic and relative. For instance, the truth between man and man. But Christian truth is neither a relative nor pragmatic thing. It is absolute. It does not tell us everything. But it tells us what we need to know about God. That is quite a difference. So the true Christian, for example, does not look to Greek philosophy to find out about God. The Scriptures tell us what we need to know about God.

Christ-led leaders also seek divine revelation to teach them what they need to know about man, about sin, about salvation. The problem with man is not psychology or education but rather sin. Not dealing with the sin factor is to not function as a qualified spiritual leader.

I suppose some would say this is a very narrow view of things. Yet there it stands: God's Holy Book—this criterion, this revelation that we call the holy Scriptures. A revelation that is full enough for us to spend a lifetime studying. No compromising. No modifying. No editing. Thus, the Holy Ghost says a teacher should be convinced of the faithful word and hold to sound doctrine.

Faith that is mere conformity is not faith at all.

Some believe otherwise than what I just stated. As free moral agents, they have the perfect right to believe what they want if they are willing to pay the price and take the consequences.

I do not believe in enforced faith. We should set the truth before people and warn them of the consequence of impenitence. Then we should leave them to their God and their conscience. People who are pressured to believe are not Christians at all. They bear the same relation to a true Christian as a cultured pearl bears to a real pearl, or a plastic flower bears to a flower that blooms in the garden.

Faith that is mere conformity is not faith at all. Our fathers' faith is not an efficient, operative faith until it becomes our children's faith. Merely to believe something because you were brought up in a church indicates that you are taking your beliefs secondhand and borrowing your convictions. Borrowed convictions do not mean a thing.

I will not rest until our fathers' faith becomes the faith of our sons and daughters.

Incongruent Beliefs

More and more people, even those in the church, hold that the Bible is not a fountain from which truth proceeds. That it is not a criterion against which religious ideas may be judged. That it is not a valid revelation with authority, but it is something else. This is a strange incongruity indeed, because, as I stated, many of these people are in our churches and are forgetting that the very idea of having a church grows out of the New Testament.

People believe the Bible is a book of moral myths. This is the kindly language some use about our Holy Book. It has some validity and some usefulness, they say, but it is not sound, and it certainly is not absolute.

Others believe the Bible is an inspiring book, a comforting book, but not a fountain out of which all truth flows. Each Sunday, these people assemble to quote from a Bible they hold as not trustworthy. They pray to a God they read about in a book that they do not believe. They seek to bring in the kingdom of heaven, which they have heard about in the book they no longer believe. They bury their dead and still quote the words, "I am the resurrection and the life."

I consider this infinite nonsense, and I understand what Jesus meant when He said, "I know your works, that you are neither cold nor hot. I could wish you were cold or hot. So then, because you are lukewarm, and neither cold nor hot, I will vomit you out of My mouth" (Revelation 3:15–16).

Either what Christ said is true, or it is not true. If it is true, we are under severe obligation to believe it, and if we believe it, we are instantly responsible to obey it. If it is not true, the whole concept of church is false, and every time we enter a church and put a dollar in the offering plate, we contribute to the falsehood and help propagate error. For Scripture says, "If Christ is not risen, your faith is futile; you are still in your sins! Then also those who have fallen asleep in Christ have perished. If in this life only we have hope in Christ, we are of all men the most pitiable" (1 Corinthians 15:17–19).

Again, I grant a person the right to be an unbeliever. But I cannot find it in my heart, nor are there any wells of charity deep enough within me, to respect someone who goes to church and at the same time does not believe in the deity of Christ, who founded the church. Nor do I respect the person who slavishly follows a watered-down version of a Bible that they do not hold to be the true Word of God. I would rather they boldly lay their Bible down and walk into the sunshine, breathe deeply, and say, "From here on, I'm on my own." The weak hang around churches whose Christ is not Christ and whose God is not God and whose Bible is not considered true.

I thank God I can say, "Now Christ is risen from the dead, and has become the firstfruits of those who have fallen asleep. For since by man came death, by Man also came the resurrection of the dead" (1 Corinthians 15:20–21).

And yet, if I believe I know everything, it disqualifies me from really being used in Christ-led situations. I am not to proudly puff out my chest and say, "I am better than you." I say, just as a poor little toad or rabbit might say, "Thank God that the sun shines on the meadow and the pond this morning, but I did not make the sun or the pond. God made both."

Leaders who think they know everything cannot lead like Christ. The sun shines because God made the sun to shine. So you and I can say, "I thank Him reverently that the sun is shining upon me this morning—that the light of truth has reached my heart. I believe in the Book, I believe in the Christ of the Book, I believe in the gospel that flows out of the Book, and I believe in the reality of our fathers' faith."

Some people will say of us, "You're so sure of yourself. You think you are holier and better than me." But how little they know of the true Christian. How little they know that you and I feel we are the worst of all humanity in our hearts, not worthy of being a Christian, and that Jesus Christ, out of His mercy and grace, has saved us. The best Christian knows if he had his own deserts, he would be in hell this hour. He knows it, and he believes it, so all the praise goes to the one who made the sun, not to the one upon whom the light shines.

God Speaks

After our Lord rose from the dead, Peter said, "God has made this Jesus, whom you crucified, both Lord and Christ" (Acts 2:36). He showed himself alive after His passion by many infallible proofs.

Hebrews 1:1–4 says,

> God, who at various times and in various ways spoke in time past to the fathers by the prophets, has in these last days spoken to us by His Son, whom He has appointed heir of all things, through whom also He made the worlds; who being

> the brightness of His glory and the express image of His person, and upholding all things by the word of His power, when He had by Himself purged our sins, sat down at the right hand of the Majesty on high, having become so much better than the angels, as He has by inheritance obtained a more excellent name than they.

People say, "I'm confused; Christianity has so many doctrines." Yet, not by any doctrine preached by a mortal man will God judge His people or judge any people at the last day. He will judge us according to what we have done with the light received: "The word that I have spoken will judge him in the last day" (John 12:48).

Our Lord Jesus laid this on the line forever when He said, "If anyone wills to do His will, he shall know concerning the doctrine, whether it is from God or whether I speak on My own authority" (John 7:17).

Some do not believe the authority of God's Word and say it is a comforting book but false in spots—what nonsense. Why would I seek immortality from a man who could not get out of his own grave?

Believe God's Word, accept the truth, and put Jesus Christ before your eyes. And as you obey Him and believe Him, seek the truth. But seek it within the Bible, not outside it.

To lead like Christ, you must understand this foundation.

Dear Father in heaven, Your truth has transformed my life more than I could ever praise You for. I pray that the truth that flows into me will also flow through me to touch those around me. I commit myself completely to Your truth. Amen.

11

Lead like Christ

MAINTAINING A TIGHT GRIP ON THE WORD

Holding fast the faithful word as he has been taught, that he may be able, by sound doctrine, both to exhort and convict those who contradict. For there are many insubordinate, both idle talkers and deceivers, especially those of the circumcision.

Titus 1:9–10

To lead like Christ, we will need to deal with hard things. It is not easy to be involved in spiritual leadership, which is why Paul warned that a "novice"—a new convert—should not be an overseer in the church, "lest being puffed up with pride he fall into the same condemnation as the devil" (1 Timothy 3:6). A novice wouldn't be able to handle many of the situations that arise for leaders.

It is essential to deal with issues that compromise biblical leadership. Too many people are willing to compromise to get along. This is not something Jesus did, and it certainly is not something the apostle Paul did.

We need sound doctrine and a tight grip on the Word of God. This does not mean knowing all of the stories in the Bible. We need to know what the Bible teaches and how it affects our lives today.

We need to address hard things, because as Paul wrote in Titus 1:10, "There are many insubordinate." In the King James, it reads, "There are many unruly." Honestly, I am sorry I have to deal with this, because I'd much rather talk about the happy side of things. Still, we live in a world of sin and the devil, where the church is like a flock of sheep in the wilderness, surrounded by wolves.

Wouldn't it be an ideal world if there were no unruly persons? No idle or vain talkers or deceivers anywhere? A place where the truth just grows without cultivation, with no weeds to cut down or hard ground to break up with a hoe, where everybody smiles and receives the Word and begins to obey it?

Indeed, it would be a comfortable, beautiful world, but you and I know that it's not that way. Maturity requires that we deal with things as they are, not as we wish they were.

I honestly think well-meaning people try to make Christianity weak and watered down. They look at the world with one eye only—the good eye. They see the sunset, but never the storm. They hear birds sing, but never the vulture. They see rosebushes, but their blind eye will not look at the thorns. They hear happy laughter, but not the moan. They see the joyous Christian but will not acknowledge the presence of the insubordinate, the idle talker, the deceiver.

That is spiritual immaturity. If I were in severe trouble and needed prayer, I wouldn't send for a man who had the reputation of never facing reality. I wouldn't want to send for too happy of a man, because in a world like this, if you are too happy, you are probably spiritually immature. The immature man sees only the happy things and doesn't see or face the other side.

Paul was a mature man who saw both sides. From prison, he wrote, "Rejoice in the Lord always. Again I will say, rejoice!" (Philippians 4:4). But Paul also described himself and other ministry workers as "sorrowful, yet always rejoicing" (2 Corinthians 6:10). I would want to pray with me the man whose heart was buoyed by the inward lift of God's life, but whose heart was also heavy with the world's grease. That is a mature Christian.

The Insubordinate and Idle Talkers

According to Donald Spence, the famous Bible expositor and dean of Gloucester in the late nineteenth century, the unruly person has these four counts against him: He refuses all obedience, acts for himself, is fatuous (silly and pointless), and is insubordinate.

The defiant man imagines he's strong, but he's not; he's just carnal. And he will allow himself to go on in that way—defiant, headstrong, and self-willed, which hurts only himself. Scripture says that even Michael the archangel, when disputing with the devil about Moses's body, didn't dare say, "I defy you." Instead, he said, "The Lord rebuke you!" (Jude 1:9).

The insubordinate also scorns the spirit of the flock, of which we are members. He refuses the shepherd's voice, and the undershepherd's, and boldly states his personal opinion against the pastor and all the godly Christians in the church.

It was this state of heart that kept ancient Israel in constant turmoil. They were always backsliding. Tearfully bruised and beaten, they would repent, be restored, and then get defiant and headstrong and go down again. The whole history of Israel was like that. It's a tragic thing that even when the Messiah came, they defied Him. They said, "We won't have this man to rule over us."

The insubordinate are restless and uneasy spirits who quote Scripture for their purpose. They're empty talkers "whose mouths must be stopped," Paul wrote (Titus 1:11). Now, some might ask, "Why not let them be?" Those who believe in the "letting alone process" point to the parable of the wheat and the tares and say, "Let both grow together until the harvest" (Matthew 13:30). They want to overlook the weeds and let everything grow together. But Jesus never taught, "Let the weeds grow in the church." In Luke 10:3, He said, "I send you out as lambs among wolves." Thus, sheep and wolves can live together in the world, but not in the sheepfold. See the difference there. The two must not live together in the church. Why? Because the unruly subvert whole houses. The word *subvert* means to overthrow by undermining morals and destroying allegiance or faith. That is why Paul says unruly, vain talkers must be silenced.

Christ's House

In the days of Paul, believers had not yet begun to build church houses. They met in synagogues, people's homes, upper rooms, wherever they could be together.

In Acts 12, after James was slain with the sword, Herod took Peter, intending to slay him too, but Scripture says prayer was made continually unto God for Peter, and God sent an angel and turned Peter loose. Where do you suppose he lit out for? To find the church, of course. He knew that they were meeting and praying for him in the house of Mark's mother, Mary.

That was a church meeting in a house, which is why Paul said to the saints, "Greet the brethren . . . and Nymphas and the church that is in his house" (Colossians 4:15). Paul also talked about preaching the gospel from house to house, or as we might say, from church to church. So the word *house* meant the church.

There are Christians now who, if we point out a church, say in shock, "Don't you realize that the church is the body of Christ, and that building is just a building?" Sure, we know that, which is why we should never let words become our master. When I say the Third Presbyterian Church or First Baptist Church, everybody knows I don't mean the building. I'm referring to the people.

Take these examples, starting with the expression "A motion was made from the floor." What is meant by that? Does it mean the people standing on the floor or sitting on chairs made the motion? It certainly doesn't mean the floor made the motion. When we say there will be a board meeting, we don't mean four pine boards will meet in the pastor's study. Originally, a group of leaders *did* sit around a board, so the word extended from the actual board where they met to mean the *people* around that board. A similar example is the House of Representatives. When someone reports that the House has not yet passed a bill, it doesn't mean the building there in Washington, DC. It refers to the several hundred elected officials who sit in that house.

Let us not get enslaved to words.

Our Defense against Deceivers

So what are we to do with the insubordinate, the idle talkers, and the deceivers? How can we deactivate them and make them harmless?

Scripture says we should respond by setting forth the faithful word and sound doctrine, convincing and exhorting so that any efforts to subvert the church are harmless. The only perfect defense against error is truth, and the only defense against a big lie is a big truth.

In Titus 1:12, Paul essentially said, "You Christians there in Crete, look out, and you teachers, be sound in the faith and careful. Hold the faithful word, because, remember, Cretans are always liars."

Paul indicted a whole group. You might wonder if a sweeping generalization like this was possible. Remember, great cities have gone completely rotten. Look at Sodom and Gomorrah. They had gotten so rotten, only half a dozen people got out. But is it possible a whole population can be corrupted?

Look at the flood. The world had become so morally corrupt that the only thing God could do was to drown them all except eight people He picked out who had yet a bit of decency left in them.

When I was a kid, we didn't have refrigeration, so we had to do what we could to keep our fruit good. Sometimes a box of apples would rot so completely that you could stick your hand into the mush all the way to your elbow. I didn't mind this, so I used to reach in and feel around. If I found a hard apple, I would take it out and wash it off. You can believe this or not, but amid the rot, there would often be one completely sound apple because there wasn't a single break in its skin.

If you hold an orthodox creed that does not result in purity of conduct, then your creed is not orthodox.

Paul taught that Christianity comes with two things: sound doctrine and sound morals. I don't believe you're sound until you have both; therefore, sharply rebuke those who are unsound in either area. For there is only one standard for Christianity—the standard of Christ—whether we are in a primitive forest somewhere or in Chicago. Don't bother with a person's customs, but when it comes to moral questions, we should bother them. If we don't, we're not preaching the Word.

When Paul said "sound in faith," he meant orthodox in belief and pure in conduct. The one brings out the other, and you can't separate the two. If you only hold an orthodox creed that does not result in purity of conduct, then your creed is not orthodox.

The ideal is not to accept arbitrary moral standards, such as "You shall eat this, and you shalt not eat that; you can wear this, but you can't wear that." Rather, let the truth purify us. Christ is the truth, and Christ is holiness incarnated. We are under obligation to be disciples of His in belief and in practice, and to worship in spirit and in truth.

Yes, even in the middle of a rotten city like Chicago, God can feel around and find some apples that are shiny and red-cheeked and sound, kept that way by God's wonderful power. And all the time we're in that same barrel, the power of God can keep us through faith by salvation, ready to be revealed at the last time, so that we never even smell the world around us.

How wonderful. Within the church of Christ, there should be no rot. Christ's church should be a place where every apple is sound and every Christian is pure.

I praise You, O Father, for Your Word that is the foundation of my life and ministry. May I never lose my grip on Your Word, and may the Holy Spirit flow in me and through me by Your Word. Amen.

12

Lead like Christ

A COMMITMENT TO SOUND DOCTRINE

But as for you, speak the things which are proper for sound doctrine.

Titus 2:1

This verse represents the practical side of leading like Christ. To be faithful to our calling, we do not have the option to waver in our doctrine. The culture may not like the doctrine, and it may not fit into their lifestyle, but the culture is not our Bible.

To the apostle Paul, salvation in Jesus Christ carried with it sound beliefs and practices in harmony with those beliefs. Paul knew nothing else but that. His theology had two sides to it: right beliefs and right living. One side could be considered the foundation, the other the building. Another way to think about it is that a tree's root is our theology—what we believe about God in Christ—and the tree and its fruit is our morality and right living.

So we have theology and morality, right belief and right living, all bound together. Strange that we have forgotten these days that they cannot be taken apart. If you even mention it, some will call you a legalist. But I do not mind names, so we will go on and teach what Paul taught.

The evangelical church has fallen on hard times, and thousands of people who were once true believers are turning away from the Word itself. How completely foolish to separate the root from the tree or the tree from the root. Would you consider what value a root has buried deep in the earth if it has no tree and no fruit on the tree? Would you consider how vain it would be to have a tree without a root? Just as you cannot have a tree without a root, you cannot have a root without a tree; the two go together. Think about how foolish it is to lay a foundation, digging down with a bulldozer, getting rid of all the dirt down there, shoveling it away, then laying the footings in and building the foundation up but letting it lie there with no building upon it. What good does it do? What good is theology unless it eventuates in right living? What good is the right doctrine unless it means morality, sound truth, and sound living?

Some try to build a building without a foundation. They want to live right, and yet they do not have any foundation for their building. So they push the building up and keep it inflated with the wind. The result is unsupported talk, talk, talk. We, on the other hand, tend to lay foundations everywhere and not have any buildings. But Paul, in this passage, essentially says, "Titus, see to it that you have both. See to it that people are not only well taught in sound theology, but also understand that theology without right conduct is vanity."

Right Beliefs, Right Living

In my thinking, Charles G. Finney was the greatest evangelist who ever lived, including the apostle Paul. Finney was not as great as Paul the theologian or Paul the apostle. But he was greater than Paul in the one job God gave him to do: evangelism. Finney taught boldly, saying things like, "It's all a mistake to have classes where you teach doctrine unless you make the application and say to the people, 'Now, as a result of believing this truth, this is how you're going to live. Bring your whole life into conformity with it.'" Right beliefs without right living have very little value. How are you going to have right living if you do not have right beliefs?

Christ gave a powerful illustration in Matthew that was in perfect harmony with Paul's teaching here in Titus. Jesus said, "Therefore whoever hears these sayings of Mine, and does them, I will liken him to a wise man who built his house on the rock" (Matthew 7:24).

Right beliefs without right living have very little value.

To hear the sayings of Christ, that is theology. To do His sayings, that is morality. Put another way, to hear the sayings of Christ, that is the foundation, and to do them, that is the building. Or, to hear and do the sayings of Christ, that is the roots and the tree. Our Lord never separated the two. He expected and meant the two to go together.

If every preacher for three months insisted that everybody obey what was preached from the Word, I believe we would have some revival in our land, some reformation that would last.

When you build a building in good weather, you build it knowing that the good weather will not last. When you build in July, you understand that there is a September into February. You build with a breath of air and the sun shining calmly on the meadows with the knowledge that the time will come when the wind blows at fifty miles an hour and the rain comes down in drenching torrents.

The Lord taught us about a man who built his house on a rock. When rain and floods descended, when winds blew and beat upon the house, the house stood. It did not fall, "for it was founded on the rock," Jesus said. Matthew 7:26 reads, "Everyone who hears these sayings of Mine, and does not do them, will be like a foolish man who built his house on the sand."

This is all very practical. When moral wisdom builds a house, it digs down to the rock and lays a heavy, good foundation. Moral foolishness builds on sand, and when rain and floods and wind come, which is to be expected, the house falls. This house built on sand was as carefully built as the other one, except the foundation was neglected. The man had some sort of theology, but it was not supported by the light.

There must be practical soundness in the hearing and the doing. Paul taught, "Speak the things which are proper for sound doctrine" (Titus 2:1).

"So what should we speak about?" I imagine people asking Paul.

"Should we teach belief in the Trinity?"

"Yes," Paul might have replied, "but I am not going to talk about that."

"Belief in the deity of Jesus?"

"Yes, but I am not referring to that."

"Baptism by immersion?"

"Of course," Paul might have said.

"You want us to teach about the second coming?"

"That is not what I am talking about."

"So what do you want us to teach?"

"I want you to teach it all, but what I am especially asking you to bear down on here in Crete are the things that benefit sound doctrine."

Paul's lesson for today is that we ought to begin to live like Christians. If we do, our prayers will immediately take on a new power, and our testimony will take on a new sharp edge. Our joy will immediately begin to spring up like wells in the desert, and I believe we can make an impression on humankind.

Some Orthodox brethren have begun to believe, over the last years, that if we can get some good polemic writers, that is, argumentative writers, who know how to argue with others, and get some good books arguing for the faith, we can cure liberalism. Never, my brother. The cure is to live like Christians. So I beg of you, let us begin to live the life that benefits sound doctrine.

If we are going to lead like Christ, we need to collect all doctrine together in simple harmony and then live out that doctrine in front of the people we are ministering to. That kind of life creates a hunger and thirst for sound doctrine.

My heavenly Father, how I do praise You for the doctrine presented in Your holy Word. I praise You that the Holy Spirit enables me to take that doctrine and apply it to my life each day. May I continue in Your strength to live the sound doctrine that You expect of me. In Jesus' name, amen.

13

Lead like Christ

TEACHING THE ATTRIBUTES OF GOD'S GRACE

For the grace of God that brings salvation has appeared to all men.

Titus 2:11

Keep in mind that spiritual leadership is more than just having expertise in theology. Theology is important to know, and something I recommend because it involves the study of God. But Christlike leadership rises above human knowledge and depends on the work of the Holy Spirit.

The Bible is an intelligent book. But one of the glories of Scripture is that while we should never go contrary to it, we often go beyond it.

This is what the Old Testament's prophets and the apostles of the New Testament did. They saw visions, dreamed dreams, and looked in the face of the awesome God. They heard and saw things their intellects could not equate with anything they knew or anything taught by mortal man. It all rose above the power of the mind, but it was never contrary to good, sound reasoning.

St. Anselm of Canterbury famously said, "I do not seek to understand in order that I may believe, but rather, I believe so that I may understand." This well-known line was based on what St. Augustine said: "Believe so that you may understand."

In the believer, faith always comes first. Then he can think as deeply, intensely, widely, and imaginatively as he wants because his thinking is built on the foundation of faith. He rises above reason but never above faith.

Understanding Scripture

Someone once asked Gypsy Smith, the British evangelist, what he did with Bible verses he could not understand. "The same as when I'm eating fish and come across a bone," he replied. "I just lay it on the side of the plate."

When you find a passage that is difficult to reason yet seems to contradict the plain teachings of Scripture, lay it aside. And be wary of the blazing fanatic who tells you that because you do not understand a passage, he will now enlighten you with teaching that contradicts twenty-five other passages.

Usually, in his epistles, Paul begins with heavy theology, laying the foundation with good and solid doctrine, and then builds upon it with exhortations, commandments, and urgings. We are to do this and thus, he often teaches. But early in Titus, Paul gives us reason: "For the grace of God that brings salvation has appeared to all men" (2:11).

When you study the Bible and come across a word or concept you don't understand, it is obviously helpful to find out what that word or concept means. But you can also save yourself a lot of confusion by identifying what it does *not* mean.

Titus 2:11 does not mean that everyone is to be saved. I know better than that, for the man who wrote Titus said, "Not all have faith" (2 Thessalonians 3:2). It was also Paul who said, "Evil men and impostors will grow worse and worse, deceiving and being deceived" (2 Timothy 3:13).

I also know our verse does not mean that all men have heard of the grace of God. It's true, the grace of God that brings salvation has been shown to all men, but that can leave the false impression that everybody in the whole world has heard of the grace of God. I wish this were so, but it is not.

If Titus 2:11 means that everybody has heard of God's grace, Christ would have returned long ago, and this terrible nightmare we call history would have ended. Christ would now be reigning to the ends of the earth, and no one would be wicked or sinful. From sunrise to sunset and from sunset to sunrise, no evil would exist.

So what does Paul mean here? He means that there has been a shining epiphany. Like a mighty sun in the heavens, God's grace shines on the person of Jesus Christ, our Lord, showing His love, pity, and mercy, and His willingness to die for His enemies.

This shining grace brings salvation, and that salvation is for men and women everywhere to receive it. That is what this passage means.

The Full Grace of God

The word *grace* has at least two meanings. Many see it as an attribute or quality of God. It is the love and mercy and kindness and goodwill that predispose Him to always be kind to those who do not deserve it. To be good to those who deserve only judgment and to pour out himself, His love, and even the blood of His own Son for the salvation of those that deserve nothing but hell. That is a quality of God and a characteristic of His heart.

I am aware that when I use the words *quality* and *characteristic*, I am humanizing God. But we simply cannot rise to the elevation where we can talk about God in divine terms. We have to talk about Him in human terms. Actually, there is no such thing as a quality of God or a characteristic of God. God's being has about it a unity and oneness. Anything we surmise about God that isn't found in Scripture is simply our minds, our intellects, attributing things to Him. For God dwells in light that no one can enter.

The grace of God has another meaning—one that encompasses a divine influence on the heart, an inward enabling, an active moral force.

The apostle Paul in 2 Corinthians 12 wrote that he had been praying to be delivered from a thorn in his flesh that caused him great distress. He prayed three times about it, and the third time, the Lord said, "[Paul,] My grace is sufficient for you, for My strength is made perfect in weakness" (verse 9). God was not speaking about an attribute of grace. This grace is an active, working force that enters the heart of a man and does things for him. Again, God said, "My grace is sufficient for you." He was telling Paul that this influence, this moral power within his bosom, could lift Paul above the thorn he was trying to get rid of. Paul, being a spiritually intelligent man, immediately replied, "Therefore most gladly I will rather boast in my infirmities, that the power of Christ may rest upon me." He knew the grace of God and the power of God were one.

All Is by Grace

It was a low and awful moment in the history of fundamentalism when the word *grace* lost its second meaning as a divine power working within us.

The grace of God, for most people, is seen as an attribute in God. But in Titus 2:11–12, Paul teaches that grace changes us: God's grace has appeared, "teaching us that, denying ungodliness and worldly lusts, we should live soberly, righteously, and godly in the present age."

Do I believe this? Oh, with everything in me. Nobody can sing with a worse voice and a happier heart, "Amazing grace, how sweet the sound, that saved a wretch like me."

Everything God has done since the beginning of time is out of grace. Nothing is by law; it all is by grace. The psalmist used to pray, "Hear me when I call, O God of my righteousness! You have relieved me in my distress; have mercy on me, and hear my prayer" (Psalm 4:1). He knew God's willingness to hear prayer was God's grace in operation. The very stars and sun overhead are the grace of God in operation. Nobody deserves anything from God. He owes nobody anything yet gives everybody everything, and therefore, we owe Him every gratitude in all the world.

Everything God has done since the beginning of time is out of grace.

All is by grace. God made the heavens and the earth by grace. When He laid the foundations thereof, it was by grace. When He gratified the earth with the firmament, it was by grace. When He made man upon the earth and blew into his nostrils the breath of life, it was by grace. Everything God has ever done has been out of the goodness of His heart. If the grace of God was only an attribute within God, it could never get to you and me.

No, the grace of God is more than that. The grace of God enters human hearts, and I even believe the very angels in heaven are motivated by God's love and grace in their hearts, although they will never understand it quite like you and I will.

Let us not be satisfied to keep all of God's qualities in God. Yes, there are attributes of God that no person can share. For instance, His self-sufficiency, His infinitude, and

His incomprehensibility. These attributes belong to God, and God cannot share them with creatures. But there are other attributes that God *can* share with creatures, including kindness, love, mercy, grace, goodness, wisdom.

If you believe grace saves you, but there is not a corresponding working within your heart toward holiness and righteousness, I have to tell you honestly, you probably are deceived. For the grace of God is received when a person declares, "I accept salvation by the grace of God through Jesus Christ." God smiles at this and then goes to work inside that person to produce the very graces that the New Testament is chock-full of.

The same grace by which we are saved now becomes an active force working within us to make us pure, good, and righteous.

Grace unto good works saves us. The same grace by which we are saved now becomes an active force working within us to make us pure, good, and righteous.

May God grant that we will not miss this. Let us trust Him to save us in grace, and that grace will operate through us to make us the kind of Christians that will adorn the doctrine of Jesus Christ.

May our dedication to Christian service and ministry motivate us to get the whole truth out to the people we are ministering to. It is the whole truth of grace that enables us to be everything God wants us to be.

O Lord Jesus Christ, how I praise You for the grace that You have provided for me. I have accepted it, and

I allow it to work in my life to Your honor and glory. Let me not be confused by what I don't know, but let me rejoice in what I do know by Your grace. Amen.

14

Lead like Christ
OUR TRUE VALUE TO CHRIST

Looking for the blessed hope and glorious appearing of our great God and Savior Jesus Christ, who gave Himself for us, that He might redeem us from every lawless deed and purify for Himself His own special people, zealous for good works.

Titus 2:13–14

A critical aspect of our spiritual leadership is understanding the value Christ puts on His people. Once we begin to understand how He thinks about us, it will change how we think about the people we lead and minister to.

You can tell how precious something is to a man or woman by how much they are willing to pay for it. When Paul says Christ gave himself for us, we learn how dear we are—and were—to Christ. I use both tenses here because Jesus Christ himself, being very God of very God, embodies in himself all the tenses there are.

Better still, He has no tense. The Bible teaches, "Jesus Christ is the same yesterday, today, and forever" (Hebrews 13:8). However, it is not talking about *His* yesterday, today, and forever. It is talking about ours. You and I have our past days—our yesterday—but even for the oldest of us, it is comparatively not a very long "yesterday." Then we have today, which is getting away from us fast. And finally, we have an eternal tomorrow. So altogether, our yesterday, today, and tomorrow are valid.

When we try to apply similar time to God in Christ, we invalidate its meaning, for we cannot say that God was. Indeed, all that our Lord is, He ever was, and all that He ever was, He ever will be. "For I am the LORD, I do not change," it says in Malachi 3:6.

So when we say how precious we were to Jesus, we mean how precious we *are* to Jesus. And when we say how precious we are to Jesus, we mean how precious we will always be to Jesus.

The Price Christ Paid

All through the Bible, in both the Old and New Testaments, redemption is found. Redemption involves pain, the giving of value for value, paying a price for something precious.

Our Christ Jesus paid a deep price that we might be redeemed. "Being in the form of God, [He] did not consider it robbery to be equal with God, but made Himself of no reputation, taking the form of a bondservant, and coming in the likeness of men" (Philippians 2:6–7). For a time, Christ made himself less than God, saying, "I will take upon me the form of a servant." Before, He had been in the position of the master. Now He was stooping to the position of servant.

How much more will you pay for men, O Lord?

His answer is not difficult to imagine: *I will become obedient unto death, as all the sons of men are obedient to their sins unto death. For their sakes, though, I will choose the worst death ever invented, at the cross.*

That's how much our Savior paid for us.

Saved from Sin

If you are ever tempted to think little of yourself, know that it is never a godly thing to do. If you are puffed up and think you amount to something, that is wrong too. If you overlook your sin and imagine you are good, that is wrong. If you are inclined to compare yourself with another and put yourself above the other, that is wrong. All these wrongs should be repented of and amended so that they do not occur anymore in your life.

Why did Christ give himself? The answer comes in the next phrase of our passage: to "redeem us from every lawless deed" (Titus 2:14). In the King James, it reads, to "redeem us from all iniquity."

Iniquity was our problem. We were caught in the messes of iniquity, and He gave himself to redeem us from all iniquity.

Notice the preposition in this phrase: not "in," but "from." Christ shall save His people *from* their sins. Let me repeat, any interpretation of New Testament Christianity that allows sin in human life is a false interpretation. Any interpretation of mercy or grace or justification by faith that allows any kind of sin, external or internal, to live unrebuked, unforsaken, unrepented of, is a travesty of the gospel of Christ and not the true gospel at all. He gave himself, and the price was himself, that he might redeem us unto purity and unto himself.

> *Our Christ Jesus paid a deep price that we might be redeemed.*

The one deep disease of the world is impurity. By impurity I mean anything that is unlike God. Sexual misconduct is an impurity, but contentiousness is another.

To some people, when you say, "It's a nice morning, isn't it," they will respond, "No, I don't think it is," and start an argument. If you compliment them, they will start an argument. No matter what you say, they are contentious. They live in this world by the mercy of people who are not contentious. They imagine themselves wonderful when they are merely recipients of an almost infinite amount of patience on the part of people who would like to tramp on them but do not. These contentious people are impure.

Other impurities include gluttony and slothfulness. Self-indulgence is another form of impurity. Pride is another form. Egoism is another form, as are self-pity, resentfulness, and churlishness. I have only named a few examples, but all that is not of God is impure.

You might be able to quote long passages of Scripture, but if the fire of the Holy Ghost and the Lamb's blood have not purified you, you are most miserable and will be rejected from the presence of the Lord. It will not be because of your beliefs so much as the state of your heart, though beliefs certainly need purification.

The Need for Purification

Paul says in verse 14 of our Scripture passage that God purifies "for Himself His own special people." The King James uses the phrase "peculiar people." That word, *peculiar*, has gotten into the enemy's hands and has been used to cloak some bizarre goings-on in the Christian church. However, the biblical meaning of the word has no connection to the strange, irrational, ridiculous, or foolish.

Jesus Christ is the perfect example of this. He walked among men with utmost rationality. Everything He did was as logical and clear and sane as the sunshine on the grass of a June morning. Jesus, our Lord, was the perfect example of a mind that is poised, balanced, and symmetrical and in perfect adjustment to itself. He never did or said anything or left anything unsaid that would cause the raising of an eyebrow or the wondering if He might not be quite all there.

In Christ's day, there were people who said He had a devil within Him because He healed the sick on the Sabbath day. The same thing was said by those who loved the law instead of man, those who loved text in place of children, and those who would rather hurl the evil woman into hell than see her forgiven. But read all four Gospels, and you will see not one instance where Jesus did or said anything that was not sane and completely normal and right.

Those who do irrational, ridiculous things in the name of the Lord and then flippantly say, "I am a fool for Christ's sake," have themselves to blame. You can only do for Christ's sake that which Christ told you to do. You cannot do what you want and then make it good by saying, "It was for Christ's sake." That is offering a swine on the altar of the Lord, and it will be rejected abruptly by the great God Almighty.

A Peculiar Treasure

Christians are not to be strange, not in any sense of that word. But we are called to be peculiar: "Ye shall be a peculiar treasure unto me above all people" (Exodus 19:5 KJV).

My son, for example, is peculiar because he belongs to me. I am his father. Love has made him mine in a way that logic cannot explain. Every mother knows that her daughter is the brightest, and every father knows his son is the sharpest, and every grandfather knows his grandson is the smartest.

The Lord has us as His peculiar treasure, and He is purifying unto himself a people to be His as special jewels. We see this in the Old Testament, where Israel was peculiar and different, but not in a ridiculous way. We see this in Daniel, who would not eat the meat of the Babylonians. He prayed several times a day and recognized a higher loyalty than one to Babylonian kings, and he retained that loyalty even when cast into the den of lions.

In the New Testament, Christians were also God's special jewels marked out for Him to be peculiar and different but not ridiculous or foolish.

To be a peculiar treasure unto God makes you different. You have a higher loyalty, and you recognize God's right to tell you how to live. Human philosophies come and go; religions come and go; artificial revivals come and go; healing campaigns come and go; new ideas come and go; scientific notions come and go. But all the time, good Christians have God in focus, living like Christ, doing God's will, and recognizing their loyalty ultimately belongs to Him. All this makes us different, but it does not make us foolish. It makes us right.

No one can argue against godliness and good works.

God's peculiar people sing loudly and give generously. They are zealous of good works. They pray long and work hard. The Bible knows nothing of armchair or ivory tower Christianity.

The church can silence critics with good works and in no other way. Preach doctrine, and they will try to turn our doctrines against us. Quote Scripture, and they will question the translation. But no one can argue against godliness and good works. The devil himself would not even try it. He knows better. Godliness and good works shut the mouths of everybody. Critics may take you out and hang you, but they will respect you while you die.

So here we have another beautiful passage in Titus that cannot be worn out. Our Savior, Jesus Christ, gave himself in order to redeem us, a peculiar people, from all iniquity and to purify us unto himself. Then Paul adds these words in verse 15: "Speak these things, exhort, and rebuke with all authority. Let no one despise you."

Thank You, O Father, for the love You pour into my life. My gratefulness can never rise to the level of what You deserve. I praise You for all that You've done for me. Help me to understand how much You love me. Amen.

15

Lead like Christ

THE FULLNESS OF CHRISTIAN LEADERSHIP

Teaching us that, denying ungodliness and worldly lusts, we should live soberly, righteously, and godly in the present age.

Titus 2:12

To lead like Christ demands that we understand entirely what it means to be a leader in the spiritual realm. This is not a job, but rather a commitment to Christ. And the path to this kind of leadership is absolute surrender and sacrifice to Jesus Christ.

Too many people think that all it takes to be a spiritual leader is to study hard, pass a test, get credentials, and be on their way. That may be the American idea of ministry, but it is not the biblical one.

If the grace of God has reached you, it has taught you by inward impulse. The first thing it teaches is denial. That is, it teaches us to disavow, renounce, repudiate. And there are two things mentioned in Titus 2:12 that are to be renounced: ungodliness and worldly lusts. *Ungodliness* means, of course, "impiety, irreverence, and whatever is not of God." Whatever God is not in is ungodly.

The dictates of grace teach us to deny whatever is ungodly, including what is accepted in many of our schools. We spend a lot of our time in the hands of pagans. We start in the preschool classes with finger painting, and we end up with a PhD from some university where the name of God is about as welcome as the name of Hitler would be in a Jewish synagogue.

It takes a certain amount of backbone to deny what everybody else is affirming and to affirm what everybody else is denying. Anybody who thinks a Christian is a weakling has never been a Christian or spent much time around Christians.

Any dead or dying fish can turn over on its back and float belly up in the stream, but a salmon will go over falls high as a church building. For the Christian, God's grace and God's Word unite to teach us that we are to deny ungodliness and renounce it for good.

Today, celebrities have become the saints and prophets of our day, and some practice ungodly things. The fact that widely known people practice them does not, in any way, mitigate the ungodliness. It is still ungodly, and we are to deny ungodliness.

It takes backbone to deny what everybody else is affirming and to affirm what everybody else is denying.

Even ungodliness found in classical literature and art is to be denied by the Christian. It is still dirty if it is dirty, and it is still ungodly if it is ungodly. It is not better because it is embalmed in classic art. Go to an art institute, and you will find some things there that God is not in. Every Christian needs enough backbone to be sneered at for repudiating such things.

If this sounds severe, remember what Jesus said: "If your right hand causes you to sin, cut it off and cast it from you; for it is more profitable for you that one of your members perish, than for your whole body to be cast into hell" (Matthew 5:30). It is better to go to heaven with only one eye and one hand than go to hell with two of each.

Denying Desire

The second thing Paul teaches us to deny is worldly lusts. He talked about the danger of desire also in 2 Timothy 4:2–4:

> Preach the word! Be ready in season and out of season. Convince, rebuke, exhort, with all longsuffering and teaching. For the time will come when they will not endure sound doctrine, but according to their own desires, because they have itching ears, they will heap up for themselves teachers; and they will turn their ears away from the truth, and be turned aside to fables.

The word *lust* means "desires, pleasure, longings for pleasure." The word appears often in the New Testament with modifiers, such as foolish lust, hurtful lust, fleshly lust, ungodly lust, former lust, youthful lust, lust in our ignorance, and lust that wars on our members.

Lusts are natural to fallen man. Of course, they are defended and excused by psychologists, sociologists, writers, marriage counselors, and consultants because they are natural. The Christian, however, is taught by the Spirit in his heart and in the pages of the Bible to renounce worldly lusts. When he picks up a book excusing worldly lusts, he shuts it and turns away because he has been taught inwardly and by the Book of God to do so.

God never calls us to dwell in a vacuum—to a life of sterile negativity, nothingness, not doing things, not being ungodly, not being lustful, not being unbelieving. He calls us away from those things to something else. He calls us out that He might bring us in.

A Three-Dimensional Life

Now, how should we live? Well, thank God for that excellent, positive word *live*. In this Scripture passage, Paul teaches that we are to live a three-dimensional life of sobriety, righteousness, and godliness.

Sobriety, which means "temperance and self-control," has to do with our relationship to ourselves. A person who cannot control himself is not going to make much of a Christian. Sobriety, self-control, temperance, and self-mastery are all related to this Christian dimension of living.

Then there is righteousness, your attitude toward others. The Spirit teaches us both in the Word and the heart that we ought to live righteously toward others. We do not cheat others. We do not rob others. We do not lie about others. We do not gossip about others to their harm.

Finally, there is godliness, which is marked by faith, reverence, and love. I list it here as the third dimension, but our attitude toward God actually comes first as a Christian. God is first, my neighbor next, and I am last. That is the way it is supposed to be in the Christian life.

Men and women who do not deny ungodliness and worldly lusts are confused and mixed up. They may join the church, but they cannot have godliness if they do not deny worldly lusts. They may join the church but not have sobriety, temperance, or self-control. If they do not have godliness and sobriety, how are they going to have righteousness?

A Radical Life

There are people today, living in lust and sinful self-indulgence, who look down on the old Puritans and men of God who used to say, "Let's do right even if the heavens fall." Our church fathers and others had extreme and radical beliefs. Lot was a radical in Sodom; Noah was a radical before the flood; Daniel was a radical in Babylon; Martin

Luther was a radical in Germany; John Wesley was a radical in England's rotten society. They were seen as radical, but they were sober, were full of the Spirit, and controlled themselves.

Someone once said, "What a cold and colorless life you have being sober and righteous and godly." That person was mistaken.

They want us to believe the beautiful people out in Hollywood are superior to our serious-minded fathers, whom they now mock. Want to get your faith up and get your heart helped? Go to Plymouth, where our fathers landed, and read their tombstones. Do not forget that this nation was whittled out by men who held God in reverence, held their neighbor in loving affection, and held themselves in control.

Our hospitals were founded mostly by this kind of person. The very word *hospital* comes up out of religious context. Almost every alleviation of human suffering known in modern society sprang up from sober, righteous, godly people. When the human heart goes free and the human mind runs away, we have atom bombs, hydrogen bombs, bacteriological warfare, and cities' destruction.

Renounce your chains and take all the infinite, limitless liberty of God.

Let me be clear, the Holy Spirit is not calling us to sit around solemnly like an owl in the daytime, staring unseeingly ahead, waiting for the end. The Lord is calling us to live—to live soberly and live righteously. The word *righteous* is not negative; it is an explosive, dynamic, positive word. The man who determines to live righteously in this unrighteous world will have a full-time job. Feel like you have nothing to do? Live righteously in an unrighteous world, and you will have something to do.

Paul calls us to renounce, but renounce what? Renounce your chains and take all the infinite, limitless liberty of God. Renounce your darkness and take all the shining light of God.

Consider what the great reformer William Cowper wrote in his poem "Song of Mercy and Judgment": "Sweet the sound of grace divine; sweet, the grace which makes me Thine." The grace of God teaches us to be good people, loving people, generous and kindly people, God-fearing people, and people with temperance, self-control, and sobriety.

It is my sweet delight, O God, to live a life of godliness by the Holy Spirit's power. Daily, as I walk toward those heavenly gates, I rejoice in the grace and strength You give me to renounce everything in my life that is contrary to You and Your nature. Amen.

16

Lead like Christ
HOW GOD SEES US

For we ourselves were also once foolish, disobedient, deceived, serving various lusts and pleasures, living in malice and envy, hateful and hating one another. But when the kindness and the love of God our Savior toward man appeared . . .

Titus 3:3–4

A significant aspect of Christ-led leadership is to understand ourselves from God's point of view. The next step is to understand how God sees the people we minister to. If we can't get that dual perspective, we certainly will not lead like Christ.

Too often, spiritual leaders see themselves and the people they are ministering to through the eyes of the culture in which they live, which seriously compromises the kind of leadership needed today.

Informed by the Holy Spirit, Paul gives us a view of our state in this section of Scripture. Titus 3:3 is like plunging into ice-cold water: "For we ourselves were also once foolish, disobedient, deceived, serving various lusts and pleasures, living in malice and envy, hateful and hating one another." Titus 3:4 is like stepping into nice warm water: "But when the kindness and the love of God our Savior toward man appeared."

We might not like verse 3, but if we do not have it, we cannot have verse 4.

Few are humble enough to read Titus 3:3 and say, "That's me." A man might say, "That is my wife"; a wife might say, "That is my husband"; a child might say, "That is my mother"; for we always have someone else in mind when it comes to things like this. I tell you frankly, I also do not think verse 3 fits me by nature. But the nicest person must accept the verse as a reasonable facsimile of his or her photograph: foolish, disobedient, deceived, enslaved to lust, pleasure-mad, living in malice, envious, and hateful. That is the description the Holy Ghost gives of us, and if we do not believe we are as bad as He says we are, we cannot believe that He is as good as He says He is.

Then, in verse 4, comes a glorious little word with such a variety of meanings—the simple word *but*.

> But when the kindness and the love of God our Savior toward man appeared.
>
> Titus 3:4

But is one of the most powerful words in the entire Bible, because it often signals repentance, rescue, deliverance, or salvation. And in this passage, a thousand things come between verse 3 and God's rescuing power in verse 4.

God's Lovingkindness

I'm not sure I know too much about the future life, since I know so little about this life. So I am very cautious about describing heavenly scenes. I am also very cautious about quoting God unless I quote from the Scriptures themselves. Still, imagine entering the Celestial City, and you see walking toward you a man you recognize because personality persists in the world to come. Do not think of yourself in heaven as a ghost or a zombie. You are going to be you, only glorified. You are going to be recognizable. You will call to memory things that happened below, just like Jesus did after He came out of the grave and remembered what He had told them while still with them before His crucifixion. You remember the last time you saw the man now coming toward you; he was cross-eyed drunk. There are little gaps in his history you do not know about, but you believed he had lived and died that way.

"You're here?" you ask.

"Yes, I am," he says with a smile before shaking your hand.

"But how did you get here? Last time I saw you, you couldn't even stand up. You were a hopeless alcoholic. Every warden and cop in the state of Illinois knew you. Now here you are. How do you account for this?"

With another smile, he answers, "Yes, but after the kindness and love of God our Savior appeared toward me, something happened."

When Christ was on the cross, don't you suppose that many people there didn't know Him as the Savior? But later on, after they heard the gospel, it is easy to imagine hundreds of Romans became believers.

I imagine that in heaven many a Roman walked up to the repentant thief and asked, "You're here? I remember when you were crucified for insurrection and thieving and all sorts of sins."

"I was all you say I was," admitted the thief. "And I was guilty of things the law never knew of. I was much worse than anybody here knows. Only God knew how bad I was, but my Savior's kindness and love appeared to me, and by a flash of spiritual intuition I recognized Him as He died there between us two. I said, 'Lord, remember me.' And He said, 'Today you will be with Me in Paradise.'"

Some people will be in heaven we never thought would be. They will get there the only way possible, and we will not know how it happened because we lost track of them.

There is nothing startling about the statement "the kindness and the love of God our Savior toward man appeared," because we know it is true. If I said, "The ocean is vast," nobody would bat an eye. If I said, "The rain that falls from heaven is wet," nobody would respond. They would wonder why I said the obvious. If I were to say that the sun is bright, nobody would say a thing.

So, when I talk about God's kindness and love, no Christian will bat an eye at that. We have heard it all our lives. That is nothing to wonder at, because that is the kind of God He is.

Incidentally, that is why unbelief is so wrong. It refuses to believe that God is the kind of God He is. When believers talk about the kindness and love of God, our Savior, there is nothing to excite attention because we know God is kind and He is love. That is what we expect.

You would expect a loving, tender mother to get up in the middle of the night and look after her baby. So when Mrs. Jones gets up at two in the morning and gives her baby a bottle, nobody will run to give her a medal. That is simply the way she is.

We know the kindness and love of God, but the text here says, "Toward man." What kind of a man? Why do our Savior's kindness and love appear to a foolish man, a disobedient man, a deceived man, an enslaved man, a pleasure-seeking man, a malicious man, an envious man, a hateful man?

This is why the love of God suddenly turned aside and flowed in its fullness toward that thief on the cross. This is why we have so many great hymns such as "Amazing Grace." What is it that amazed the man? That God was gracious? No. The wonder lies in that the kind, gracious love of God should have for its object such a slavish, foolish, disobedient, deceived, lustful, malicious, envious, hateful person as I am.

This is why hymn writers still have us singing about the wonderful love of God toward man.

Why Does God Love Us?

David asked our Lord, "What is man that You are mindful of him, and the son of man that You visit him?" (Psalm 8:4).

Some scholars tell us that *mindful* means "a fixture in the mind." So the only eccentricity of our great, perfect God is that He loves mankind with a fixture He cannot escape. He cannot shake it off. Even our hating one another has not discouraged God, nor changed His mind in the slightest about us.

So why does God love us? I would suggest three thoughts here that might help you intellectually if not spiritually.

The only eccentricity of our great, perfect God is that He loves mankind with a fixture He cannot escape.

The first reason is that God is love and only does what is natural to Him. It is natural for the sun to shine, we say. It is natural for birds to fly and fish to swim. It is natural for that which is love to love. So we say God loves us because it is the natural thing for Him to do.

The second reason God loves us is that we are His creatures, and He is pleased with everything He made. When sin came in and ruined it, God started over to remake it, but He still loves us. Apart from sin, we are a part of His creation.

There is a third reason: We are made in His image. But I do not make this as a statement but more as a question. Could it be that the great God who sinlessly and perfectly loves himself sees the tattered fragments of His own image in the fallen man, loves himself in the man, and seeks to redeem the man because that man has a family resemblance?

Now, don't go away thinking I am certain about this third reason. It is a question: I wonder if God loves himself in us. We must still be born again to be saved, for Paul wrote:

> According to His mercy He saved us, through the washing of regeneration and renewing of the Holy Spirit, whom He poured out on us abundantly through Jesus Christ our Savior, that having been justified by His grace we should become heirs according to the hope of eternal life.
>
> Titus 3:5–7

Notice we have been made heirs, which means we inherit everything God has. If you find being an heir of God hard to believe, it is because you do not see yourself in verse 3: someone who is "foolish, disobedient, deceived, serving various lusts and pleasures, living in malice and envy, hateful and hating one another."

If you do not believe you are as bad off as this, you will never believe that you are as well-off as a recipient of grace, because psychologically it cannot be done. If you hold out on God and do not confess how bad you are, your nature will not permit you to take all the promises about how good God is to you. You must see how bad you are to see how good God is and how wonderful His grace is.

To understand what it means to be an heir of God, imagine a little boy who has lived in the slums of some great city—New York, perhaps. He is eight or ten years old and has lived among ash cans in alleys, sleeping in corners and ducking policemen after stealing fruit from corner stores. He's never had a new shirt or pants or shoes in his life.

Suddenly, somebody comes along and adopts him off the street corner. It's one of the richest men in America, with yachts and big cars to run around in. We tell the boy, "You know what? You're an heir. This man has adopted you, and now you have ranches in Arizona and Canada and huge estates up and down the coast of Florida. It's all yours, to say nothing of money in the bank." The little fellow cannot comprehend it, though, and would exchange all of it for a Popsicle.

We are heirs of God according to the promise of eternal life.

God does not blame us for similar thinking. We are used to spiritual poverty. We are used to locking up everything, shutting our door, and nervously wondering, "Did I lock it?" We are used to living in the "slums" of the universe. Then suddenly, somebody throws cold water on us and says, "You're an heir of God." We shake our heads and say, "Well, I'm willing to believe it, but I haven't the faintest notion what you're talking about."

Read your Bible, study it, pray, and keep learning to think the way God thinks. Maybe someday you will know a little bit. If you do not know it here, you will know it in heaven. We are heirs of God according to the promise of eternal life.

The dynamic of my spiritual ministry is to understand how God sees me and how God sees the world around me. In my leadership I transfer this passion for God's vision to the people I am ministering to.

Dear heavenly Father, I rejoice in You although I do not understand all there is in You. I cannot comprehend that, being who I am, You would love me. I do not understand it, but I accept Your love and long for You to transform me into Your image. Amen.

17

Lead like Christ

THE CHRIST-CENTERED SERVANT

This is a faithful saying, and these things I want you to affirm constantly, that those who have believed in God should be careful to maintain good works. These things are good and profitable to men.

Titus 3:8

If, as spiritual leaders, we are to be "profitable to men," as Titus 3:8 says, we need to understand our position with Christ. We are to be Christ-centered servants, which means everything we do should flow out of that center. Anything in our lives that compromises that center needs to be dealt with and removed immediately.

To be a Christ-centered servant means we will have quite a bit of suffering along the way. It will not be easy, and none of it will come naturally. It will come from the Holy Spirit's work flowing from the center of our life, which is Jesus Christ.

As addressed earlier in this book, Paul instructed Titus and us to "speak the things which are proper for sound doctrine" (2:1). This was followed by exhortations for older men and women, and young men and women. Older men, Paul said, should be sober, reverent, and temperate. Likewise, older women should be reverent. Young women, Paul said, are to be discreet, chaste, homemakers, and good. Young men, sober-minded and reverent.

Fifteen verses later, we read: "These things are good and profitable to men" (3:8).

What Is Good?

A lesson in semantics is not needed, nor a lesson in English, but look at that word *good*. "These things are good," Paul writes. The word *good* has a long list of meanings in the average dictionary. It is one of those workhorse words that you can get on and ride anytime because it means so many things. Here, the thought of morality is not present. When Paul says these things are good, he does not mean the things are morally good, virtuous, or as right as something can be. What he means is these things are valuable to you. They are to your advantage and profit. That is what he means by "good," which in the Greek is also used in the parable of the sower: "Other [seeds] fell on good ground."

"Good ground" does not mean ground that is moral or virtuous. A hunk of earth cannot be morally good. Turned-over sod cannot be virtuous, but it can be valuable and profitable.

When a doctor sees a sick man and says, "You need to take this treatment. It won't be pleasant, but it will be good for you," that is a good thing. It is good in the sense that it is advantageous and profitable to the man.

We say to a hungry child, "Here, eat this. It will be good for you." The child eats, nourishing her little body, and pretty soon her eyes begin to shine again and color comes back to her face. Good food makes the little one healthy again.

We say to an intelligent young man, "It is good for you to finish high school." Later, when he comes around again and asks, "Now that I have finished high school, what should I do?" we respond, "Well, you're intelligent. I believe you are college material; it will be good for you. Go on to school and learn." We do not mean the college will be a morally good place, although it should be. We mean that if he studies certain subjects, they will profit him.

When people approach us, it is not unusual that they are hoping to profit from the encounter. The person who tries to sell you something is not so much thinking about you; he hopes it will be good and profitable for him.

When we arise to the everlasting and eternal, we will see how beautiful and how solemn it all is and realize that the good and profitable things of everyday life are short-term. The sick man who got treatment and recovered will eventually die. The hungry child who ate food and got her health back will die after a while too. The student will wither away and cease to learn after college or university. The profit is only for a time.

Good and Profitable Forever

When God approaches us with an expectation, a command, He never comes saying, "This will be good for me." Instead, He says, "These things I say to you are good and profitable to you *forever*." God always thinks in terms of eternity and forever. Isn't it a solemn and wonderful thought that you possess something time cannot wear out?

Think with me about the eternal soul of a Christian. Consider his faith. What matters to him? What affects him? God Almighty made him of a different material altogether. He lives differently; he is of another matter altogether. God essentially says, "I've given you that which cannot wither, cannot die, cannot be seen." God made the earth, He made man upon it, and He willed vigorously and actively the good of that man.

God wants the full development of my soul, and He makes the appropriate preparation for me to be in fellowship with Him forever. *This is good and profitable for you*, He tells us. If we would only know this deeply, we would realize that God's will is not something to fight, but something to accept joyously. It would change our lives.

After God made Eden, He planted a garden eastward. As He showed it to the man, I am sure He expressed, "This is good and profitable for you." Then God pointed out certain fruit and said, "Now, these are all for you. Look at them hanging on all these trees. That one, though—don't bother it because of my reasons. But all the rest of the garden is yours; it is good and profitable to you." Adam and Eve disobeyed and sinned, though, and God cast them out of the garden. Why? Because it was good and profitable for them to not remain there. God put the man and woman out where they could be fluid, malleable, and changeable, where He could get hold of them and turn them back from their sinful state to holiness.

Of course, the man and woman mourned their trip out of the garden. John Milton, in his epic poem *Paradise Lost*, portrayed them walking away from the gate of the garden, looking pensively over their shoulders at what had once been their happy home, and going into the world. But it was good and profitable for them that they should. That's always God's way: "This is good for you; this is profitable for you."

This was true all through the Scriptures. When God instituted sacrifice and redemption, He said, "Here, slay this animal, put the blood on the altar, and confess your sins, for that is good and profitable for you." Later on, when the time came for Mary to have her baby and name Him Jesus, God announced to all, "This is good and profitable for you." When the boy Jesus opened His mouth and taught in the temple, it was good and profitable for the teachers. And when He died on the cross, if people had eyes to see, they could've seen written in letters of fire: "This is good and profitable for you."

The devil's powerful lies are that God looks upon man seeking to find fault and to punish and to harm. The devil brought that dirty, scandalous lie to Eve and got her to sin.

He has been telling the same to Eve's children from that hour to this. "There sits God on the throne, the great bully," the devil says. We are weak and short-lived, and the devil has eternity to pull his weight around and turn the minds of people against God. But he forgets that God gave man free will and said, "This is good and profitable for you." God gave man the world and said, "It's good and profitable for you." God sent His Son to die, raised Him from the dead, set Him at His right hand, and said, "This is for your profit. This is for your good." If we could only remember and know this, that God is always speaking of our good and our profit.

Through Sorrows and Tribulations

The Lord sometimes puts a little pressure on us. He allows sorrow and pain and loss and tribulation to come, but He wants us to know, "This is good for you, and I'm thinking of your profit."

The modern notion that Christianity is one massive Sunday school picnic with a swim thrown in is all wrong. The Christian life is reasonably happy. And if you live close to God, it is a very happy life. But it is still a life shot through and through with sorrows and hardships and pains and tribulation. Know that sorrows and tribulation are not God's highest will, for there will not be any of them in heaven. In this mixed-up world, though, we are in a state where they are necessary.

Why is it so hard to get people to do what's good for them, yet easy to get them to do what is sweet and pleasurable, whether it's good for them or not? Why is it that when there is a choice between the flesh and what is good for us, we choose the flesh ninety-seven times out of a hundred? Why is it that when God gives us a choice between the present and eternity, a vast, overwhelming number of people choose the present? Why?

I think an enemy has done this, and I know his name. The devil has done it—that evil one who hates us.

Because we are so badly fallen, we almost every time choose short-range pleasure over long-range benefits. When there is a choice between God and the flesh, almost every time the flesh wins and God loses.

Only now and again does God find someone bold enough and faith-filled enough to forego short-range benefits and instead take long-range promises. Moses was one such person. He despised the court of Pharaoh in order to claim the long-range promises of God. In Hebrews 11, you will see a long list of others who spurned short-range benefits and took eternity and the long-range profit that God provides. Remember that God gives you choices and will sometimes say, "Now, this doesn't appear so good, but it is good and profitable unto you." Let us learn to take the thing that is good for us rather than the thing we like. Let us learn to suffer it out and battle it through.

People today are suffering tragically and will not get one bit of blessing out of it. To encourage himself and others, the great South African pastor Andrew Murray, while suffering from back pain, once wrote, "In time of trouble say . . . He will make the trial a blessing, teaching me the lessons He intends me to learn, and working in me the grace He means to bestow."[1]

1. Andrew Murray, quoted in "'In Time of Trouble Say' (Andrew Murray)" by Vance Christie, *VanceChristie.com*, August 29, 2015, http://vancechristie.com/2015/08/29/in-time-of-trouble-say-andrew-murray/.

People pour their sorrows and griefs out to me. I see many trying to escape their hardship and plow around it. It's too bad.

Whether the world or the flesh or the devil makes a proposition, always remember it is for your pleasure for a short run. God may send something that is not so pleasant, but it is for your good and your profit as the ages roll. Learn to choose the hard way if it is God's way.

I recommend you let all this sink in. Let these truths soften you and prepare you for eternity, because you are going there one of these days. You are going there the easy fleshly way, having lived a life of artful dodging of the cross and artful escaping of tribulation. Or you are going there like a Christian on the road to the Celestial City, wearing his armor and carrying his sword with his bow under his arm, ready to face any dragons, lions, or devils that are in the way.

Despite what the devil says, always remember that what God tells you is good for you. If you do not like what God directs, do it anyway and thank Him. Do not grumble, do not complain, do not go through life gloomy. Thank Him for everything, and say,

---

Father, this is not particularly enjoyable, but I will enjoy it anyway, knowing that You sent it and that it is good and profitable for me. Amen.

18

Lead like Christ

OUR MOTIVES REVEAL CHRIST'S CHARACTER IN US

Avoid foolish disputes, genealogies, contentions, and strivings about the law; for they are unprofitable and useless. Reject a divisive man after the first and second admonition, knowing that such a person is warped and sinning, being self-condemned.

Titus 3:9–11

It is rather depressing to be reminded that people have not mended over history. Paul wrote his letter to Titus approximately 1,900 years ago, and we are still having foolish disputes about spiritual matters. Human nature has not changed.

In this section of Titus 3, Paul also talks about avoiding genealogies related to the law. Our modern minds may not understand the significance of this, but family trees were important to Jewish leaders because Scripture taught that the Messiah would be "the Son of David" (Matthew 22:42)—an ancestor of Abraham. They kept page after page of genealogies, so if a man claimed, "I am Christ," they could go to the records and check his family history.

But you know religious people; they cannot let things be.

They started to misuse the genealogies, making them into a puzzle and coming up with fanciful interpretations. Rather than trusting Scripture, they looked for a deeper meaning of Abraham begot Isaac, Isaac begot Jacob, and Jacob begot Joseph, and Paul sought to protect the church from these foolish disputes.

A Sincere Heart

In Psalm 8:4, David asks the Lord, "What is man that You are mindful of him?" The more I study humanity, read the Word, and pray, the more I am convinced that one thing everybody needs to be converted is sincerity. Even the most sinful and corrupt person, if he chooses to be sincere for five minutes in God's presence, can be delivered. There is nothing the blood of Jesus Christ cannot cleanse, nothing God will not forgive.

It is insincerity that curses mankind. And people with foolish disputes and genealogies simply are insincere. A man may have high morals, but if he is insincere, God cannot save him. If a man is sincere and looks to Jesus Christ, though, he can be converted.

There is nothing the blood of Jesus Christ cannot cleanse, nothing God will not forgive.

This applies to our approach to the Scriptures. Our motives must be to reverently seek God's will, to seek holiness of heart and life, to seek to know Christ intimately, and to learn how to instruct others to do the same.

These are the only reasons to go to the Scriptures. If I go to the Scriptures to try to find Sputnik, I am guilty of foolishness and unprofitable questions, which can only be vain in the end. But if I go to the Bible, with reverence and prayer, to find how I can do God's will and be holy, then God will honor me and accept me as a sincere man. If I am not a good man but a sincere man, He will get busy making me good soon enough.

Paul also talked about genealogies and sincere motives in his letter to Timothy:

> Nor give heed to fables and endless genealogies, which cause disputes rather than godly edification which is in faith. Now the purpose of the commandment is love from a pure heart, from a good conscience, and from sincere faith.
>
> 1 Timothy 1:4–5

The whole purpose of the Bible, Paul wrote, is to love out of a pure heart, a good conscience, and a sincere faith. And he was determined to not allow any neat little tricks of interpretation to ensnare his people. He wanted them to be a holy people.

Psalm 1:1–2 reads: "Blessed is the man who walks not in the counsel of the ungodly, nor stands in the path of sinners, nor sits in the seat of the scornful; but his delight is in the law of the LORD, and in His law he meditates day and night."

There are teachers who say some psalms are messianic and that this introductory psalm is a picture of Jesus Christ. But do you know what that interpretation does? It instantly relieves me of all responsibility. It is not any of my business to see that I walk not in the counsel of the ungodly, nor stand in the path of sinners, nor sit in the seat of the scornful. I'm free from all responsibility.

Then there is 1 Corinthians 13, that wonderful and terrible chapter that gives me more trouble than any other chapter in the entire Bible. Some teachers say verse 1 is also a description of Jesus:

> Though I speak with the tongues of men and of angels, but have not love, I have become sounding brass or a clanging cymbal.

If this describes Jesus, you and I have no obligation toward it at all. But 1 Corinthians 13 was never written as a description of Jesus. It shows how Christians are to love. Until Christians have done everything that we know how to do in prayer, in surrender, and in faith to have this kind of love in our hearts, we have been simply tricked by a wrong interpretation of this chapter.

Imagine, if you will, a man who has the gift of tongues and the gift of prophecy, feeds the poor, and is willing to give his body to be burned as a martyr. He can do all of this and yet still have a bad motive and no love, and it will profit him nothing. The easy way to get rid of this is to make it be about Jesus Christ.

I do not want to be abusive. I want to be kind. I preach this because I believe that these verses in Psalm 1 and 1 Corinthians 13 are also for me. I am going to labor and pray that these passages describe me as well as describing Jesus Christ our Lord.

Dealing with Others

Paul says in Titus 3:10, "Reject a divisive man after the first and second admonition." In the King James Bible, the man is described as a heretic.

As understood in our day, a heretic is a false teacher. He does not teach the truth. By picking out certain things in Scripture, he builds and teaches a fabric of untruth. But that is not what *heretic* meant when Paul used it. In Greek, the word *heretic* means somebody who, for any reason, is resentful and offended, who has hurt feelings, who sometimes gathers a few malcontents around him and makes a little group of quiet rebels who don't go along with the crowd, or with other Christians. People like this are not false teachers. They are dividers, troublemakers, injurious critics.

The word *reject* here means to shun or avoid, and, as the text says, it should not happen until after the first and second admonition. You don't immediately throw out a divisive man. Give him a quiet admonition, maybe a second one, and if he doesn't change his ways, then you avoid him. This is in harmony with the words of Jesus in Matthew 18:15–17, where He says that if someone sins against you but won't listen to your admonition, you should go to the person again with some others, then take it to the church if necessary, and if the person still refuses to listen, "Let him be to you like a heathen and a tax collector."

Titus 3:14 says: "And let our people also learn to maintain good works, to meet urgent needs, that they may not be unfruitful." Paul could not stand idleness or irresponsibility. He could not stand slothfulness or unfruitfulness. I imagine that when Paul saw a tree with no fruit on it, his heart ached. He wanted fruit on that tree. Likewise, when Paul came across a Christian who was just twiddling his thumbs, Paul would immediately sit down and write a firm epistle, saying, "Get up, get going, go to work. Let the Word of God get you moving. Do not simply sit in an ivory tower and be a Christian in your head. Get down to business and be useful."

The Witness within Us

In John Bunyan's classic book *The Pilgrim's Progress*, Hopeful, Christian, and other pilgrims need to cross a river. When old Christian almost sinks, Hopeful basically says, "I found a sandbar, come on," and pulls him onto firmer ground. Pretty soon they all get to the other side of the river where there is a great gate to the Celestial City.

After Christian and Hopeful are invited into the city, a self-important, cocky pilgrim named Ignorance, who had fallen behind the group, knocks at the gate and says, "Open up, I'm here."

"Where's your certificate—your credentials?" asks an old man at the gate.

"What? I don't have any."

"All right, then. You will go down."

And with that, Bunyan closes his great book with these awful words: "Then I saw that there was a way to hell, even from the gate of heaven."

Many people travel the Christian highway but do not have in their heart the credentials of a true believer. They only think they do, and when this earthly life is over, they will find themselves going from the gate of heaven to hell.

Do not take your witness for granted. If within your heart there is sincerity, humility, and faith, God will build a wall around you and send His angels to guard you. But as soon as you start taking your faith for granted, look out. See to it that God has accepted you and that you have His witness within. Live with Paul's closing words to Titus in mind: "Grace be with you all. Amen."

As I travel my journey, O God, I look to You for my motivation, and I trust You for my credentials to serve You until I enter into that Celestial City. Amen.

19

Lead like Christ

FACING SPIRITUAL WARFARE

Jesus said to them, "Because of your unbelief; for assuredly, I say to you, if you have faith as a mustard seed, you will say to this mountain, 'Move from here to there,' and it will move; and nothing will be impossible for you. However, this kind does not go out except by prayer and fasting."

Matthew 17:20–21

One subject I have not yet expounded on in this book is spiritual warfare. Lct me step out of the book of Titus to focus on what Jesus said about spiritual warfare. Read through the Gospels and follow the ministry of Jesus, and it is hard not see how much spiritual warfare He encountered.

Spiritual warfare is a significant part of leadership today. Too often, though, it is either ignored or overly emphasized. And when people focus on one thing to the exclusion of everything, heresy results.

Behind spiritual warfare is the devil. Look at this scenario in the book of Luke.

> Then Jesus, being filled with the Holy Spirit, returned from the Jordan and was led by the Spirit into the wilderness, being tempted for forty days by the devil. And in those days He ate nothing, and afterward, when they had ended, He was hungry.
>
> Luke 4:1–2

It might be hard to imagine this, but we need to understand that the enemy trying to destroy us is the same enemy who tried to destroy Jesus in the wilderness. But notice it says that Jesus was "led by the Spirit into the wilderness." Ask the Holy Spirit to lead you as you engage in spiritual warfare.

Later in Christ's ministry, His disciples were asked by a man to heal his son from seizures brought on by a demon.

It was the first time they had faced spiritual warfare, and they failed.

After Jesus cured the child, the disciples asked, "Why could we not cast it out?" Jesus explained, "This kind does not go out except by prayer and fasting" (see Matthew 17:14–21).

If you study Scriptures about the devil's workings, you will see that he does not often duplicate his attacks. As he tried with Jesus in the wilderness, he tries to create unique situations for our failure.

As spiritual leaders, we need to prepare ourselves and our people for spiritual warfare. To disregard the opposition we face is to put ourselves and the people we are ministering to in grave danger. We must never take anything for granted in the spiritual realm.

Our Resources

I believe the first thing is to know the resources needed to deal with the spiritual warfare before us.

The key is what Jesus said to the disciples: "This kind does not go out except by prayer and fasting." We must be committed to prayer and fasting now. The significance here is that we are to be warfare ready—praying to prepare ourselves *before* the enemy attacks.

A favorite Old Testament story is the one of David and Goliath. If you've been in Sunday school, you've probably heard this story a hundred times.

You might remember that King Saul tried to prepare David to face the champion enemy, Goliath, by equipping him with armor and a bronze helmet. I say, if King Saul thought his equipment could defeat the enemy, why didn't he face Goliath himself?

Unlike King Saul, David had the spiritual understanding to realize that only God can equip us to battle the enemy. David took off the armor and helmet and instead took five stones and a sling for his encounter with Goliath. It certainly looked like an unequal face-off. As Scripture says, "Then David said to the Philistine, 'You come to me with a sword, with a spear, and with a javelin. But I come to you in the name of the Lord of hosts, the God of the armies of Israel, whom you have defied'" (1 Samuel 17:45).

It is tempting to try to equip ourselves to match the enemy, but that does not lead to victory. In our spiritual warfare, we need to come at the enemy "in the name of the Lord of hosts."

What bothers me about this scenario is that David was a teenager, and King Saul allowed him to go before an enemy ten times greater than anybody in Israel's army at the time, knowing that if David lost, the Philistines would win the whole battle. This needs to be a concern for us as leaders. If we lose a battle to the enemy, many people will be affected by it.

If we fail, there will be collateral damage. But when we succeed, there will also be collateral damage. By that I mean, there will be damage whether we win or lose.

For example, when we stand up against the enemy, there will be friends, or people we thought were friends, who will run away from us. They want to compromise with the culture because it has infiltrated their very lifestyle. I feel sad about the people who have walked away because we, as the church, stood against some aspect of the enemy. I have a hard time explaining that except to say they were carnal Christians and deeply rooted in the culture around us.

Not a Solo Effort

I need to point out very clearly that spiritual warfare is not to be undertaken by leaders only. Yes, David faced Goliath alone. And yes, we face our own Goliaths alone. But it needs to be a priority for every spiritual leader to bring others together to stand against the enemy.

We need to preach the Word as Paul emphasizes in the book of Titus and as I have tried to outline in this book. We need to preach the Word so that our people will be equipped with the necessary armor to face the enemy.

The apostle Paul says, "Put on the whole armor of God, that you may be able to stand against the wiles of the devil" (Ephesians 6:11). This is to be a daily exercise for every believer.

As a Christlike leader, I am responsible for training my people in spiritual warfare and putting on the armor of God. If we don't put on the armor of God, we will be vulnerable to "the wiles of the devil." He knows which buttons to push and how to take advantage of our weaknesses.

It needs to be a priority for every spiritual leader to bring others together to stand against the enemy.

This is why we believers need to assemble, because we are in spiritual warfare and need each other. For one thing, most Christians work in places where there are few Christians. Some are in situations where they are the only Christian, and I'm sure this has a negative effect on them. That's why when we come together, we do so to encourage one another and to pray for one another.

If the enemy can keep us from gathering, he has a platform to plant seeds of despair in the believer's life. And believe me, this is the enemy's agenda.

One of the great problems in leadership, particularly in the area of spiritual warfare, is overconfidence in self. There are many conferences to help us build up our belief that we can do what God has called us to do if we just put our mind and heart to it.

But if we can do what God has called us to do in our strength, why do we need God?

God has a record of not calling the equipped, but rather equipping the called. An Old Testament story that exemplifies this is the one about Gideon. God called Gideon to deliver Israel from the Midianites. God did not call Gideon because he had what it took to do the job. No, there was something in Gideon that God could work upon, and He could equip him to do it.

God is not looking at us to use us because of what we can do in our human strength. He is looking for a vessel through which He can work to accomplish His purposes. The less I can do in my own strength, the greater God's opportunity is to work through me for His honor and glory.

When Gideon realized God had called him to do this job, he did not believe he had the qualifications. The task before him was greater than he could handle. Gideon represents the average Christian that God wants to use for His purpose.

Gideon's response to God—"If You will save Israel by my hand" (Judges 6:36)—was not a sign of lack of confidence in God, but rather a lack of confidence in himself. I think Gideon was saying, *Why would you choose me?* Gideon wasn't trying to build up his own confidence. He was desirous of understanding God's confidence in calling him. You need to have absolute assurance that you understand what God is calling you to do.

This led Gideon to essentially say, "If you're calling me to do this, then let me put fleece out, and by morning if the fleece is wet and the ground around the fleece is dry, I will believe you."

The interesting thing is, God was not intimidated by Gideon's lack of confidence. The next morning the fleece was exactly the way Gideon had described.

Gideon's counterpart in the New Testament was Thomas. Many know him as doubting Thomas, but I am not sure that really applies to him. When he told the other disciples he needed to see Christ's wounds to know He was alive, Thomas was simply saying, "Unless I see I cannot believe." And this did not in any way intimidate Jesus, because the next week Jesus appeared and complied with Thomas's request.

When Gideon saw what happened to the fleece, he still was not sure that he was the one God could use, so he asked God to reverse the challenge and make the fleece dry and the ground around it wet. Once again, the next morning it was exactly the way he had asked God to make it.

All of this helped Gideon convinced himself it was God's calling, not his own heart, to save Israel. The battle before Gideon was greater than Gideon; therefore, he wanted to make sure he understood what God was going to do.

As spiritual leaders, we often take on battles that God is not calling us to. We take on cultural battles and political battles and financial battles, all to show people around us what mighty men and women of God we are.

Confidence in Christ

We need more spiritual leaders with Gideon's confidence, not in themselves, but rather in the God who is calling them. To understand God's call has nothing to do with our abilities. It has everything to do with God's will, and He is selecting us to complete that will in His strength.

How many Christians struggle with trying to find out God's will? They place it upon their education, experience, abilities, and networking. They believe God will do a work through them by using their strength and skills.

In the great spiritual battle set before us, God is not looking for men and women who qualify according to religious opinions. He is looking for people who are willing to surrender themselves entirely to God and allow God to direct them in the direction He wants them to go. This is God's battle, not ours.

O God and Father of the Lord Jesus Christ our Savior, may I surrender to Your desires in order to be used by You to do the work You want done. My confidence in myself is minimal, but my confidence in You is unlimited according to the Holy Spirit's work in my life. Amen.

CONCLUSION

As you have given time to read through this book, I hope your heart has been stirred to be a true servant of Christ and lead like Christ in the situation where God has placed you.

We cannot select where we will serve. That is the prerogative of God, who created us and redeemed us for ministry unto Him. If I am where God wants me to be, I will have the Holy Spirit's power and authority to do work for His honor and glory and pleasure.

Leading like Christ is not an easy thing. To truly lead like Christ, we need to understand who Christ is and His aspirations concerning the church.

One thing that drives me to my knees these days is what I see happening in the church of Jesus Christ. The culture has all but taken it over. Our church leaders bow humbly before the culture, and we are paying the price for that.

I pray that this book will help leaders have the backbone needed to do what is necessary for the church of Jesus Christ today.

To lead like Christ will cost us everything. The apostle Paul made this clear when he said, "From now on let no one trouble me, for I bear in my body the marks of the Lord Jesus" (Galatians 6:17). How dare we expect the world to treat us any differently than it treated the apostle Paul.

Read about Paul in the New Testament, and you will discover the suffering and persecution that he endured because of his stand for Christ. Let us not be afraid of this. If we bow to the culture, we are turning our back on Christ.

In the Old Testament, Shadrach, Meshach, and Abednego's response to King Nebuchadnezzar should be a pattern for us. When the king demanded that they bow to the government or else go into the fiery furnace, they replied,

> "If that is the case, our God whom we serve is able to deliver us from the burning fiery furnace, and He will deliver us from your hand, O king. But if not, let it be known to you, O king, that we do not serve your gods, nor will we worship the gold image which you have set up."
>
> Daniel 3:17–18

This kind of commitment is needed today. We will face our own fiery furnaces when we serve God and lead like Christ. But the great joy in persecution is that we will experience God's grace like never before.

We should expect the same kind of persecution that came to Christ, the apostle Paul, Titus, and all the followers of Christ down to this time. We are marching toward heaven, and the enemy will do anything he can to keep us from going forward victoriously.

That sly old devil cannot keep me from going to heaven, but he can rob me of the victory along the way. If I understand his agenda, I will keep my eyes focused on leading like Christ in whatever situation I am presently in.

If the devil can rob me of my victory, the people I am ministering to will also be robbed of victory. I am not only standing for myself, but I am also standing for them. When I minister to them according to Christ's agenda, I will have Christ's power and authority to do so.

As you have read this book, my prayer is that you have humbled yourself before God and put whatever your Isaac is on the altar and allowed Christ to be your one and only authority in your life and ministry. I pray you will be an example, as Titus was, of leading like Christ in the ministry that you are in right now.

O God and Father of the Lord Jesus Christ, I pray that each one that has gotten this far in this book will have had layers of surrender to the Holy Spirit in their ministry. I pray they will be willing to turn their back on the world and follow Christ regardless of the consequence. I pray that the people they are ministering to will begin to see Christ in the one who is leading them. O Holy Spirit, may You be able to operate as You choose in the lives of these who are surrendering to You today. This I ask in the precious name of Jesus Christ, whom we serve. Amen and amen.

A.W. Tozer (1897–1963) was a self-taught theologian, pastor, and writer whose powerful words continue to grip the intellect and stir the soul of today's believer. He authored more than forty books. *The Pursuit of God* and *The Knowledge of the Holy* are considered modern devotional classics. Get Tozer information and quotes at www.twitter.com/TozerAW.

Reverend James L. Snyder is an award-winning author whose writings have appeared in more than eighty periodicals and fifteen books. He is recognized as an authority on the life and ministry of A.W. Tozer. His first book, *The Life of A.W. Tozer: In Pursuit of God*, won the Reader's Choice Award in 1992 by *Christianity Today*. Because of his thorough knowledge of Tozer, James was given the rights from the A.W. Tozer estate to produce new books derived from over four hundred never-before-published audiotapes. James and his wife live in Ocala, Florida. Learn more at www.jamessnyderministries.com and www.awtozerclassics.com.

You May Also Like . . .

Pulled from A.W. Tozer's sermons, this book captures his teaching on God's will for your life. We all face tough decisions, but Tozer's biblical insight will help guide you on the right path. In the same way that God led His people out of Egypt into the promised land, this book will help reveal where God is leading and reassure you that He is by your side.

A Cloud by Day, a Fire by Night

Enjoy the collected wisdom of one of the most beloved Christian authors in history with this seminal guide, ideal for fans, pastors, ministry leaders, and Christian writers. Arranged topically, this quick reference will open your eyes to the depth and insight of Tozer's thoughts on popular culture, the nature of God, spiritual warfare, God's Word, and more.

The Quotable Tozer